THE BLOCKADE
Runners and Raiders

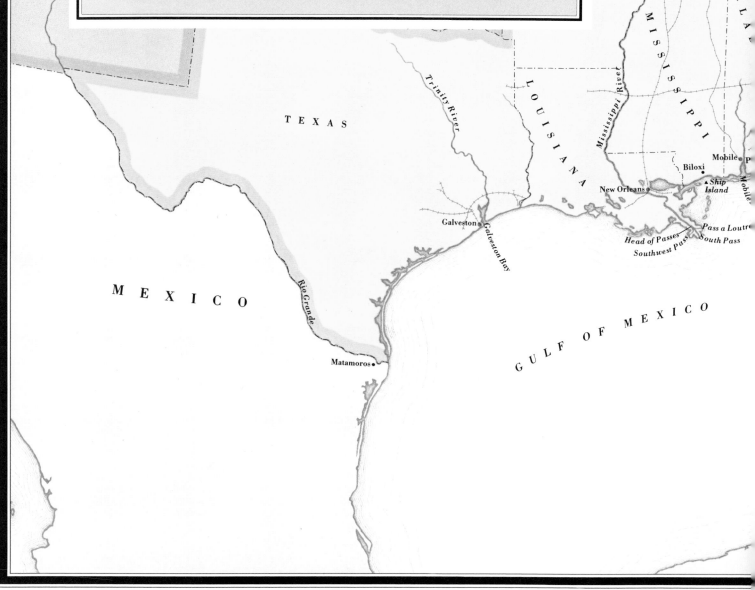

A SEA WAR OVER CONFEDERATE TRADE

The Civil War at sea was essentially a battle over commerce vital to the Confederate States. Attempting to cut off Southern exports and European imports, the United States Navy blockaded much of the Atlantic and Gulf coasts, concentrating on seven major Southern ports (*red dots*) connected by railroad or navigable river to the Confederate interior. In retort, Southern shipowners and British entrepreneurs set up extensive blockade-running companies. Eluding the Federal squadrons, runners carried their cotton cargoes to neutral ports in Bermuda, the Bahamas and Cuba; there they loaded up for the return trip with European war matériel delivered by transatlantic merchantmen.

Behind this struggle were several related operations. Early amphibious landings were staged by Federal forces to seize strategic Southern points for use as bases (*triangles*) to support the blockade. The Confederates and Federals built and deployed ironclads to break or defend the blockade. And in the courts and shipyards of England and France, ministers, consuls and secret agents for both sides vied for ships and war matériel.

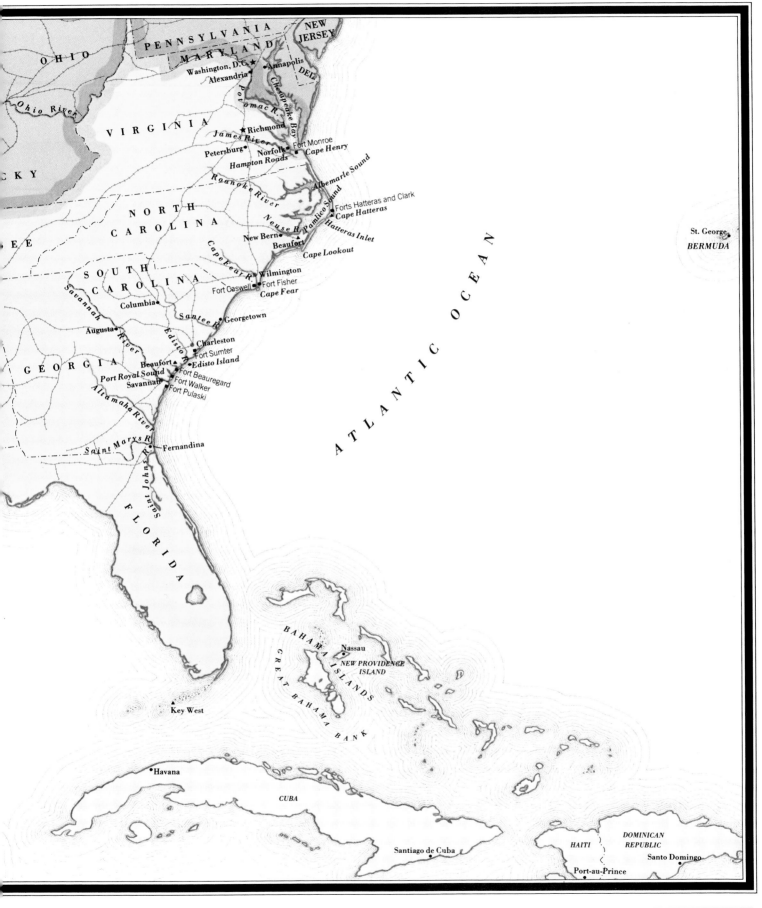

OHIO

PENNSYLVANIA

NEW JERSEY

MARYLAND

Washington, D.C. ★ •Annapolis

DEL.

Alexandria•

Potomac R.

Chesapeake Bay

VIRGINIA

James River ★ Richmond

Fort Monroe

Petersburg• Norfolk• *Cape Henry*

Hampton Roads

Roanoke River

KY

Albemarle Sound

NORTH CAROLINA

Forts Hatteras and Clark

Pamlico Sound *Cape Hatteras*

Neuse R. *Hatteras Inlet*

New Bern• Beaufort•

Cape Lookout

E E

SOUTH CAROLINA

Cape Fear R. Wilmington•

Fort Fisher

Fort Caswell• *Cape Fear*

Columbia• *Santee R.* •Georgetown

Savannah River Augusta•

Edisto R. •Charleston

Beaufort• •Fort Sumter

Port Royal Sound •Edisto Island

Savannah• Fort Beauregard

GEORGIA Fort Walker

Fort Pulaski

Altamaha River

Saint Marys R. •Fernandina

Saint Johns R.

FLORIDA

St. George• *BERMUDA*

A T L A N T I C   O C E A N

BAHAMA ISLANDS

Nassau•

NEW PROVIDENCE ISLAND

GREAT BAHAMA BANK

•Key West

•Havana

CUBA

Santiago de Cuba• *HAITI* *DOMINICAN REPUBLIC*

Port-au-Prince• Santo Domingo•

Scale of Miles

0   50   100   200   300   400   500

This volume is one of a series that chronicles in full
the events of the American Civil War, 1861-1865.
Other books in the series include:

The Cover: The ironclads *Merrimac (left)* and *Monitor*
duel at Hampton Roads, Virginia, amid helpless wood-
en warships of the United States Navy. The epic battle
on March 9, 1862, dashed Southern hopes of breaking
the Union blockade off the Atlantic coastline.

For information on and a full description of any of the
Time-Life Books series listed on this page, please call
1-800-621-7026 or write:
Reader Information
Time-Life Customer Service
P.O. Box C-32068
Richmond, Virginia 23261-2068

THE
CIVIL
WAR

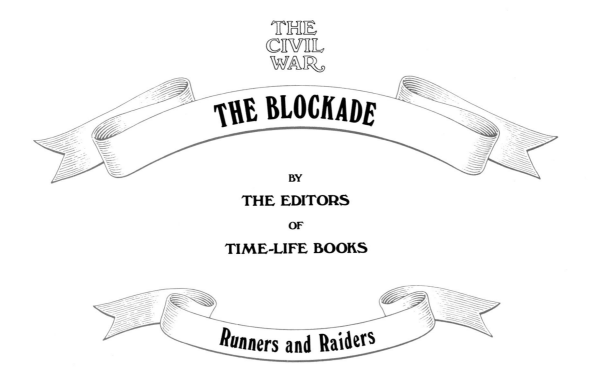

THE BLOCKADE

BY

THE EDITORS

OF

TIME-LIFE BOOKS

Runners and Raiders

TIME-LIFE BOOKS, ALEXANDRIA, VIRGINIA

TIME-LIFE BOOKS

EDITOR-IN-CHIEF: Thomas H. Flaherty

Director of Editorial Resources: Elise D. Ritter-Clough
Executive Art Director: Ellen Robling
Director of Photography and Research:
John Conrad Weiser
Editorial Board: Dale M. Brown, Janet Cave, Roberta
Conlan, Robert Doyle, Laura Foreman, Jim Hicks,
Rita Thievon Mullin, Henry Woodhead
Assistant Director of Editorial Resources: Norma E. Shaw

PRESIDENT: John D. Hall

Vice President and Director of Marketing:
Nancy K. Jones
Editorial Director: Russell B. Adams, Jr.
Director of Production Services: Robert N. Carr
Production Manager: Prudence G. Harris
Supervisor of Quality Control: James King

Editorial Operations
Production: Celia Beattie
Library: Louise D. Forstall
Computer Composition: Deborah G. Tait (Manager),
Monika D. Thayer, Janet Barnes Syring,
Lillian Daniels
Interactive Media Specialist: Patti H. Cass

Time-Life Books is a division of Time Life
Incorporated

PRESIDENT AND CEO: John M. Fahey, Jr.

The Civil War
Editor: Gerald Simons
Deputy Editor: Henry Woodhead
Designer: Herbert H. Quarmby
Chief Researcher: Philip Brandt George

Editorial Staff for *The Blockade*
Associate Editor: Jeremy Ross (pictures)
Text Editor: R. W. Murphy
Staff Writers: Adrienne George, David Johnson,
John Newton
Researchers: Erin Taylor Monroney, Clara E. Nicolai
(principals); Harris J. Andrews, Kristin Baker,
Charlotte Marine Fullerton, Gwen C. Mullen
Assistant Designer: Cynthia T. Richardson
Copy Coordinators: Allan Fallow, Anthony K. Pordes
Picture Coordinator: Eric Godwin
Editorial Assistant: Annette T. Wilkerson
Special Contributors: Peter Chaitin, Brian McGinn,
James Street Jr.

Correspondents: Elisabeth Kraemer-Singh (Bonn);
Margot Hapgood, Dorothy Bacon (London); Miriam
Hsia, Lucy T. Voulgaris (New York); Maria Vincenza
Aloisi, Josephine du Brusle (Paris); Ann Natanson
(Rome). Valuable assistance was also provided by:
Juliette Tomlinson (Boston); Jill Rose (London); Felix
Rosenthal (Moscow); Nicki Kelly (Nassau, Bahamas);
Carolyn Chubet (New York).

The Consultants:
Colonel John R. Elting, USA (Ret.), a former Associate
Professor at West Point, is the author of *Battles for Scandinavia* in the Time-Life Books World War II series and of
The Battle of Bunker's Hill, The Battles of Saratoga, Military History and Atlas of the Napoleonic Wars and *American Army Life*. He is also editor of the three volumes of *Military Uniforms in America, 1755-1867*, and associate editor
of *The West Point Atlas of American Wars*.

James I. Robertson Jr. is C. P. Miles Professor of History
at Virginia Tech. The recipient of the Nevins-Freeman
Award and other prizes in the field of Civil War history, he
has written or edited some 20 books, which include *The
Stonewall Brigade, Civil War Books: A Critical Bibliography* and *Civil War Sites in Virginia*.

William A. Frassanito, a Civil War historian and lecturer
specializing in photograph analysis, is the author of two
award-winning studies, *Gettysburg: A Journey in Time* and
*Antietam: The Photographic Legacy of America's Bloodiest
Day*, and a companion volume, *Grant and Lee, The Virginia Campaigns*. He has also served as chief consultant to the
photographic history series *The Image of War*.

Les Jensen, Curator of the U.S. Army Transportation
Museum at Fort Eustis, Virginia, specializes in Civil War
artifacts and is a conservator of historic flags. He is a
contributor to *The Image of War* series, a freelance writer
and consultant for numerous Civil War publications and
museums, and a member of the Company of Military Historians. He was formerly Curator of the Museum of the
Confederacy in Richmond, Virginia.

Michael McAfee specializes in military uniforms and has
been Curator of Uniforms and History at the West Point
Museum since 1970. A fellow of the Company of Military
Historians, he coedited with Colonel John Elting *Long
Endure: The Civil War Years*, and he collaborated with
Frederick Todd on *American Military Equipage*. He has
written numerous articles for *Military Images Magazine*,
as well as *Artillery of the American Revolution, 1775-1783*.

Clark G. Reynolds, curator of the museum aircraft carrier
U.S.S. *Yorktown* at Patriots Point, South Carolina, has
taught at the United States Naval Academy at Annapolis.
He is the author of *The Carrier War* in the Time-Life
Books Epic of Flight series, *Command at Sea: The History
and Strategy of Maritime Empires* and numerous articles on
military history.

James P. Shenton, Professor of History at Columbia University, is a specialist in 19th Century American political
and social history, with particular emphasis on the Civil
War period. He is the author of *Robert John Walker* and
Reconstruction South.

Library of Congress Cataloguing in Publication Data
Main entry under title:
The Blockade: runners and raiders.
 (The Civil War; v. 3)
 Bibliography: p.
 Includes index.
 1. United States — History — Civil War, 1861-1865 —
Naval Operations. I. Time-Life Books. II. Series.
E591.B57 1983   973.7′5   83-468
ISBN 0-8094-4708-8 (retail ed.)
ISBN 0-8094-4709-6 (lib. bdg.)

CONTENTS

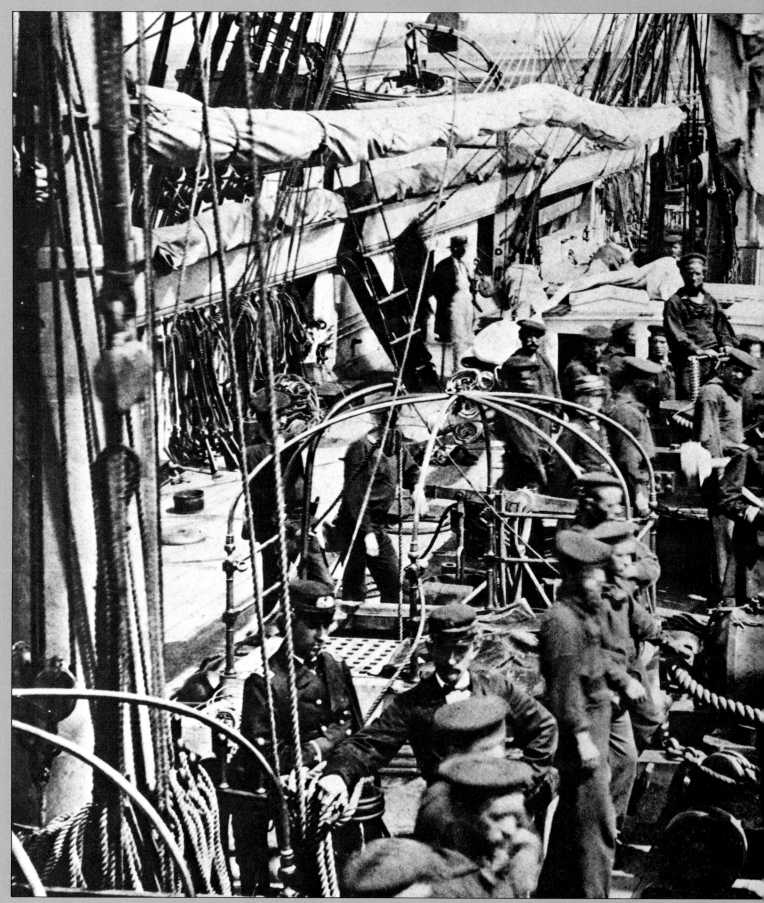

The entire 76-man crew of the U.S.S. *Huron*, captained by Lieutenant Commander Francis H. Baker (*center*), crowds the deck for review in this 1864 photograph

The sloop, powered by both sail and steam, served on blockade duty between February of 1862 and May of 1864, in which time she captured six blockade-runners.

The Year of Makeshift Navies

"It is essentially necessary that the Navy should at this time put forth all its strength and demonstrate to the country and to foreign powers its usefulness and capability in protecting and supporting the Government and the Union."

GIDEON WELLES, U.S. SECRETARY OF THE NAVY, SEPTEMBER 18, 1861

1

The United States and the Confederate States faced many urgent and perplexing problems when, with the surrender of Fort Sumter on April 13, 1861, they suddenly found themselves at war and utterly unprepared to fight. Perhaps their thorniest problem was the matter of launching a war at sea. Both Abraham Lincoln and Jefferson Davis saw that an effective, aggressive navy could play a decisive role in economic warfare and diplomatic maneuver, and surely would play an important role in supporting land campaigns. And the two Presidents knew all too well that their Navies were woefully inadequate.

The Confederate Navy was little more than a figure of speech. It had only a handful of revenue cutters, seized from Federal port authorities in the seceding Southern states, and meager personnel consisting chiefly of 237 Southern officers who had resigned their commissions in the United States Navy to cast their lot with the Confederacy. But since the Navy had been created by the Confederate government only two months before, Southerners were not surprised or dismayed by its small beginnings.

The United States Navy faced critical problems of a different kind. Years of conservative peacetime habits and bureaucratic red tape had left the fleet in poor condition. The Navy claimed only 90 warships and about 9,000 officers and enlisted sailors, and those figures grossly exaggerated its real strength. No fewer than 48 ships were out of commission, idled by lack of funds for repairs and upkeep. Though the Navy boasted a dozen fine wooden-hulled steam cruisers, more than half of its 42 operational vessels were obsolescent sailing ships, serving on past the time when steamers had proved superior in speed and maneuverability. To make matters worse, nearly every Navy vessel that could make sail or steam was off protecting American interests in foreign ports. At the start of hostilities, Lincoln had only three proper warships at his disposal.

As for the men of the U.S. Navy, they were well enough trained—though not for the war they were about to fight. They had studied foreign harbor defenses and drilled for ship-to-ship combat on the high seas, but they knew little about operations among the myriad inlets and islands of America's ragged Southern coast.

Clearly, the Union and the Confederacy needed many more ships to strengthen their weaknesses. Most of all they needed ships to attack the enemy where he was vulnerable.

One of the Union's strongest points— and, paradoxically, one of its greatest weaknesses—was its enormous merchant fleet, second in tonnage only to Great Britain's. It stood to reason that many vessels of this wide-ranging fleet could not be defended against swift, hard-hitting lone-wolf raiders, even if the U.S. Navy was hugely enlarged for escort duty.

By contrast, the Confederacy's lack of shipping was to some extent advantageous.

Master Jeff—and his Navy.

A Northern cartoon, ridiculing the makeshift Confederate Navy, shows President Jefferson Davis preparing to launch a toy ship in a barrel. The cartoon was printed on envelopes used by patriotic Northerners.

Since only 10 per cent of the prewar American merchant fleet was now owned by Southerners, the majority of Southern imports and exports would be carried in foreign bottoms. This meant that the Confederates would be able to seek out and destroy Union merchantmen with little concern for corresponding losses at the hands of Federal raiders.

Nevertheless, the Confederacy was vulnerable in its heavy dependence on foreign manufactures. Unless it developed war production of its own, the factory-poor agricultural South would have to import weapons, munitions and consumer goods of all kinds, from razors and axes to buckets and boots, and even cloth made of Southern cotton. If the U.S. Navy could cause a general and protracted stoppage of imports, it could eventually jeopardize the entire Confederate war effort. Just such a stoppage was the Union's prime objective for the war at sea.

Thus before the shooting started, both governments understood what kind of naval offensive was needed. Accordingly, in the hectic days of patriotic hysteria that followed Sumter's fall, the two Navy Departments committed themselves to a double-barreled program: shipbuilding for a long war and, for the short haul, a scramble to acquire stopgap vessels of any kind, just so long as each was big enough to accommodate a single cannon. For both Navies, it would be catch-as-catch-can through the rest of 1861.

The two governments quickly put their plans into practice and declared their strategies in the first naval-policy statements of the War. To buy time to build a genuine navy, Jefferson Davis set out to improvise a temporary one. On April 17, just four days after Sumter surrendered, Davis published an announcement inviting shipowners to apply for Confederate letters of marque and reprisal. These licenses, much like others issued by belligerent nations in the past, authorized the bearers to turn privateer and, acting as Navy vessels, capture Union merchantmen to sell for their own profit as contraband of war. The Confederate government also vowed to pay the privateers 20 per cent of the value of any Federal warship they destroyed.

Two days later, Abraham Lincoln proclaimed a naval blockade on the Confederacy, covering the Atlantic coast from South Carolina to Florida and then following the Gulf coast to the Mexican border. Soon after, as Virginia and North Carolina edged toward secession, Lincoln extended the blockade north to the Potomac River. And, in a warning against Davis' call for privateers, he stated that any private party caught in possession of a Union merchantman would be tried, convicted and hanged for piracy.

A great deal more than naval planning had gone into Lincoln's proclamations. Both he and Davis had taken great care to act responsibly and to establish the legality of their actions in the eyes of the world. The approval or disapproval of the European powers, turning on the respect or disregard shown by the Union and the Confederacy toward the body of agreements that formed international law, could have an enormous effect on such practical matters as trade, credit and material aid, and could even bring about foreign intervention in the American war. The problem was particularly acute for the Confederate States, a new government whose reliability was as yet unproved.

Was privateering legal? Davis believed that the European powers would concede the Confederacy's right to practice privateering.

This letter of marque for the schooner *Gibraltar*, issued in 1864, was one of the last such privateering commissions awarded by Confederate President Jefferson Davis. To secure a commission, a prospective privateer posted a bond of $5,000 or $10,000, depending upon the size of his crew; the money would be forfeited if he committed acts of piracy or otherwise embarrassed the Confederacy.

It was true that England and France had signed the 1856 Declaration of Paris, which disavowed privateering as a form of warfare. But the United States had not signed the declaration, and Davis held that this fully justified his own decision to use privateering against the Union.

Lincoln disputed Davis' argument on a Constitutional principle underlying the War itself. He deeply believed, and had often declared, that the Union was indivisible, and that therefore the Confederacy was not a sovereign nation, as its government asserted, but merely a collection of lawless states in temporary rebellion. Lincoln considered Confederate privateering to be piracy on the ground that Davis had no authority to license privateers, as legitimate nations might if they had not signed the Declaration of Paris.

The legal status of the Confederacy had also been involved in Lincoln's proclamation of a blockade. International law defined a blockade as an act of war against a belligerent nation. Therefore Gideon Welles, the U.S. Secretary of the Navy, had advised Lincoln against proclaiming a blockade; the proclamation would, by implication, grant the Confederacy exactly what Lincoln meant to deny it—the status of nationhood. As a belligerent nation, the Confederacy would have the right under international law to buy arms in Europe, to float loans there, to conduct business abroad subject only to the regulations of the countries involved, and to raid enemy commerce not as pirates but as a legitimate national navy. Instead, Welles had urged Lincoln to close the Southern ports by executive order; he felt sure Congress would agree.

Although Lincoln naturally endorsed Sec-

The Short, Unhappy Career of a Miscast Privateer

Privateering was a dangerous business even in the summer of 1861, when the Union blockade was temptingly inefficient. Of that, there was no clearer proof than the brief, inglorious fling of the *Petrel*. The little two-gun revenue cutter, seized from the Federals by South Carolina at the start of the War, was so unseaworthy that in May of 1861 the ship-poor Confederate Navy refused to accept her. But a group of Charleston gentlemen eagerly took the risk for a chance at huge profits. They paid for two months' worth of repairs to outfit the ship as a privateer.

The *Petrel* set out on her new career in the early-morning darkness of July 28. She slipped past the Federal warships blockading Charleston Harbor and began prowling the coast in search of prey. At dawn, her captain, William Perry, spied a sail on the horizon and ordered his 40-man crew to give chase.

Soon Perry saw that he had made a terrible error. The sail belonged not to a slow, vulnerable merchantman, but to a fast and powerful Federal frigate, the 52-gun *St. Lawrence*. The pursuer suddenly became the pursued.

By 10 a.m. the *St. Lawrence* had caught up to the *Petrel*. Perry foolishly ran up the Confederate flag and opened fire. The warship answered with a single crushing 8-inch shell that blew a gaping hole in the little cutter. The *Petrel* began to sink.

After less than half a day in business, the privateer's career had ended. And Perry and his crew, less four men who drowned, were in manacles, on their way to Philadelphia and a Federal prison.

The *St. Lawrence* fires a broadside at the Confederate privateer *Petrel* in this exaggerated portrayal of their one-shot battle.

retary Welles's view, he had heeded a strong argument against it. The British Minister in Washington, Lord Richard Lyons, had made it clear in long and detailed exchanges with Secretary of State William H. Seward that Queen Victoria's government would refuse to respect an executive order closing the Southern ports; to honor the directive would, in effect, back Lincoln's punitive measures against the Confederacy. England preferred to have a blockade declared because it wanted Southern cotton; once the Confederacy was acknowledged as a belligerent nation, British merchants would be within their rights under international law to flout the blockade and do business with the South—at their own risk.

Lincoln had realized that if the British chose to resist an executive order, they might extend diplomatic recognition to the Confederacy and send Royal Navy warships to accompany British merchantmen and guarantee their free passage to Southern ports. He had also weighed the advantages of declaring a formal blockade. It would confer on the United States the right under international law to stop and search neutral merchant ships on the high seas and to confiscate contraband of war bound for Confederate ports. All things considered, Lincoln had made the practical decision; declining to challenge England, he called his measure a blockade.

As soon as Lincoln proclaimed it, the Confederates ridiculed the blockade in the belief that Britain would help them break it. After all, they reasoned, Britain owed nothing to the North, which was its industrial and mercantile rival. On the other hand the South was an important customer for British manufactures and shipping services. Most significant, the South produced half of the world's output of a commodity that was processed voluminously and lucratively in English mills—cotton.

Believing wholeheartedly in their slogan "Cotton is king," the Confederates conceived that their exports of raw cotton made England hostage to the South. It could hardly be otherwise, they thought, since almost a quarter of Britain's population was engaged in the textile business. The owners of the great mills of England's Midlands would be ruined if the cotton supply was interrupted, and thousands of British mill hands might starve if the shuttle looms came to a halt for lack of raw materials.

Since Britain had abolished slavery, there was some British support for the Union's antislavery stand. But the most influential segments of British society endorsed the Confederate view. Even the press paid fealty to King Cotton. The humor magazine *Punch* declared in doggerel: "Though with the North we sympathise / It must not be forgotten / That with the South we've stronger ties / Which are composed of cotton." *The Times* of London, the voice of the British establishment, declared, "The destiny of the world hangs on a thread. Never did so much depend upon a mere flock of down!"

And so, in euphoric optimism, the Confederates concluded that the insatiable British need for cotton would compel England, and perhaps France also, to come to their aid with diplomatic recognition, loans and war matériel. They believed that if the blockade did choke off Confederate exports, Britain would send a fleet to break the strangle hold and ensure her steady supply of raw cotton. England's economic interest would be the guardian of the South's independence.

Going a step further, many Southerners

decided to create a cotton shortage to speed the day when Britain and France would intervene in their behalf. Local cotton brokers and state-government officials voluntarily declared a cotton embargo. Although the embargo was not official, it was backed by some acts of the Confederate Congress.

This was "cotton diplomacy" carried to a quixotic extreme, but only a few appreciated that fact. One, Confederate Attorney General Judah P. Benjamin, urged the South to ship as much cotton as fast as possible to secure credit in Europe for sorely needed weapons and munitions. But in the heady aftermath of the victory at Fort Sumter, most Southerners blithely ignored his plea.

They should have listened. Though they were gambling on a cotton shortage, an immense surplus existed. The Southern states had produced and exported bumper crops throughout the late 1850s and into the spring of 1860. This glut of cotton, combined with mounting fears of trouble in America, had led many European brokers and speculators

President Abraham Lincoln confers with his Cabinet in this composite photograph fabricated by Mathew Brady. Standing at right is General Winfield Scott, commander of the U.S. Army, whose "Anaconda Plan" for strangling the Confederacy included the coastal blockade and called for winning control of the Mississippi River.

to stockpile cotton imports from the South. More than a year would pass before the mills of England and France depleted their stocks. Indeed, British warehouses were so oversupplied with cotton that some was resold at inflated prices to Northern textile mills, relieving the shortage in the Union. And as the stockpiles dwindled, Britain and France turned to alternative sources of cotton, mainly Egypt and India.

The cotton embargo turned out to be a blunder that cost the Confederacy dearly. It forfeited incalculable revenues, and it helped the U.S. Navy do the work of blockading until the fleet was much larger and better prepared. Fortunately for the Confederacy, the cotton embargo was never more than partially effective and was gradually relaxed. But it was not until 1863 that Southerners abandoned the misguided policy.

In spite of the informal embargo, Confederate envoys busily pursued cotton diplomacy in the courts, countinghouses and back alleys of Europe. Their first test came early on. Three Confederate commissioners—William Lowndes Yancey, Ambrose Dudley Mann and Pierre A. Rost—had been sent abroad before the outbreak of hostilities to negotiate treaties of commerce and to secure diplomatic recognition from Britain, France, Belgium, Spain and Russia. These three men were not the best of diplomatists, but neither were they as bad as a report that preceded them to England. Yancey, a veteran Southern statesman and a man of considerable charm, was described by Britain's consul in Charleston as "impulsive, erratic and hotheaded; a rabid Secessionist who favors a revival of the Slave Trade." Mann, a stolid Virginian, was judged by the same consul to be "a mere trading politician pos-

sessing no originality of mind and no special merit of any description." And Rost, a former judge from Louisiana, was said to have been picked for his assignment largely because he spoke French.

In spite of these disparaging characterizations, the Confederate commissioners gained something of a victory on May 3, 1861. They were received unofficially by Britain's Foreign Secretary, Lord John Russell. Of course Russell was too suave to commit himself to anything but the time of day; he said little and listened with flattering attentiveness. The commissioners informed him that the Southern states had seceded legally and that the Confederacy was a sovereign nation determined to secure and maintain its independence. Then, fulfilling their instructions from Confederate Secretary of State Robert Toombs, they made a "delicate allusion" to England's dependence on cotton. The commissioners concluded with the hope that Britain would "recognize the independence of the Confederate States of America at an early date."

Lord Russell did offer vaguely to bring these matters before the Cabinet. But after a second meeting on May 9 he privately decided that relations with the United States, a recognized power, required him to refrain from further meetings with commissioners from an unproven government hostile to its former parent, the United States. The commissioners were soon informed that they should henceforth communicate with His Lordship in writing. The letters they sent were undoubtedly read, but the British government would not endorse any policy. The commissioners waited. They visited other European capitals and got the same put-off. Finally, on September 23, the Confederate government dissolved their commission.

Well before then, the Confederates received a much more direct and cautionary signal that their diplomatic suit would not go as smoothly as they had expected. On the 13th of May, Great Britain officially declared its neutrality.

Naturally this declaration disappointed the Confederates. But it was equally disappointing to many Northerners, who expected England to respect the Union view that the Confederacy was a lawless rebellion and, therefore, to cease trading with the South. Quite simply, Britain intended to postpone for as long as possible any watershed decision regarding the Confederacy. But in late July, the Confederate Army's rout of Union forces at Bull Run produced a slight thaw in the British chill toward the Confederacy. A hope was thus planted in Confederate minds, and it would grow, that more victories on the battlefield might yet win the Southern suit for Great Britain's hand.

Meanwhile, at home, the two Navy Departments had begun war preparations amid great confusion, crippling shortages, inadequate funding and uncertain priorities. Simultaneously they launched sea operations against the other side and competed with other branches of their own government for money and manpower. Real progress was slow, hard-won, and to a large degree the result of keen leadership by the two Secretaries of the Navy.

U.S. Navy Secretary Gideon Welles, formerly a Connecticut newspaper editor, was a curious figure whose full brown wig lent an incongruous cast to his flowing white beard and stern Puritan features. He knew little of ships or naval strategy at the time of his ap-pointment, though he had served in the Navy Department as Chief of the Bureau of Provisions and Clothing during the administration of James Polk. Lincoln had chosen Welles mainly to give New England representation in the Cabinet. However, Welles quickly showed administrative talent and a rare ability to subordinate the special interests of his department to the Union's overall strategy. He would become one of Lincoln's closest advisers, affectionately dubbed "Father Neptune" by the President.

Lincoln's luck in appointing Welles was matched by Welles's good fortune in getting Gustavus Vasa Fox as his assistant. The son of a Massachusetts physician, Fox joined the Navy as a midshipman in 1838 at the age of 16. He served during the Mexican War, but became discouraged by the slow pace of promotion in the peacetime Navy and, like many other young officers, resigned his commission to enter private business. Through a family connection with Montgomery Blair, Lincoln's Postmaster General, Fox came to the President's attention in early 1861—just in time to conceive the abortive effort to relieve Fort Sumter in April. Even though the expedition failed, Fox's careful planning and infectious enthusiasm led Lincoln to appoint him in August 1861 to the new post of Assistant Secretary of the Navy.

At first Welles was wary of his assistant, but he soon found that Fox was energetic, resourceful and loyal. Fox supplied the operational and technical background that the Secretary lacked. Though some of Welles's critics gibed that he was a puppet in Fox's hands, the two men complemented each other: Fox spun off ideas, ranging from the brilliant to the impractical, while Welles kept a steady hand on the tiller. Together, the dour

Main Ship Types of the Civil War

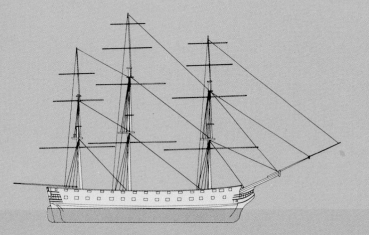

SAILING FRIGATE: U.S.S. *CONGRESS*
Launched 1841. Length: 179 feet.
Draft: 22 feet 6 inches. Weight:
1,867 tons. Guns: 50. Crew: 480.

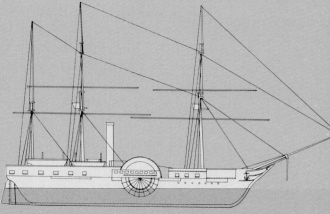

SIDE-WHEEL FRIGATE: U.S.S. *MISSISSIPPI*
Launched 1841. Length: 229 feet. Draft:
19 feet. Weight: 3,220 tons. Guns: 10.
Crew: about 280. Top speed: 8 knots.

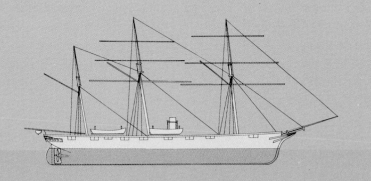

STEAM SLOOP: C.S.S. *ALABAMA*
Launched 1862. Length: 220 feet.
Draft: 14 feet. Weight: 1,050 tons.
Guns: 8. Crew: 149. Top speed: 13 knots.

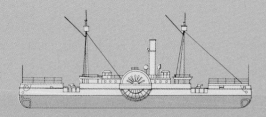

SIDE-WHEEL GUNBOAT: U.S.S. *SASSACUS*
Launched 1862. Length: 205 feet.
Draft: 9 feet. Weight: 974 tons.
Guns: 10. Crew: 145. Top speed: 14 knots.

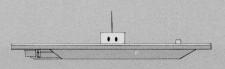

MONITOR: U.S.S. *MONITOR*
Launched 1862. Length: 172 feet. Draft:
10 feet 6 inches. Weight: 987 tons.
Guns: 2. Crew: 57. Top speed: 6 knots.

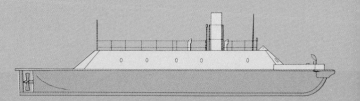

IRONCLAD RAM: C.S.S. *MERRIMAC-VIRGINIA*
Rebuilt 1862. Length: 275 feet.
Draft: 22 feet. Weight: 1,275 tons.
Guns: 10. Crew: 330. Top speed: 5 knots.

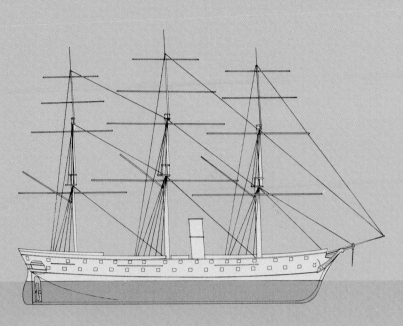

STEAM FRIGATE: U.S.S. *WABASH*
Launched 1855. Length: 301 feet 6 inches.
Draft: 23 feet. Weight: 4,808 tons. Guns: 40.
Crew: about 600. Top speed: 9 knots.

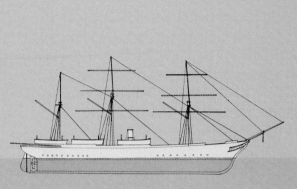

STEAM SLOOP: U.S.S. *KEARSARGE*
Launched 1861. Length: 201 feet 4 inches.
Draft: 14 feet 3 inches. Weight: 1,550 tons.
Guns: 7. Crew: 163. Top speed: 11 knots.

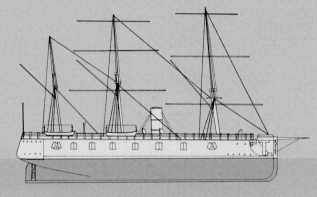

IRONCLAD STEAMER: U.S.S. *NEW IRONSIDES*
Launched 1862. Length: 230 feet.
Draft: 15 feet 8 inches. Weight: 3,486 tons.
Guns: 16. Crew: 449. Top speed: 8 knots.

SIDE-WHEEL STEAMER: C.S.S. *R. E. LEE*
Launched 1862. Length: 260 feet.
Draft: 10 feet. Weight: 900 tons.
Guns: none. Top speed: 13 knots.

IMPROVED MONITOR: U.S.S. *PASSAIC*
Launched 1862. Length: 200 feet.
Draft: 10 feet 6 inches. Weight: 1,200 tons.
Guns: 2. Crew: about 75. Top speed: 7 knots.

DOUBLE-TURRET MONITOR: U.S.S. *ONONDAGA*
Launched 1864. Length: 226 feet.
Draft: 12 feet. Weight: 1,250 tons.
Guns: 4. Crew: 150. Top speed: 9 knots.

Puritan and his ebullient aide set out to locate money, build ships, and recruit officers and men in sufficient numbers to transform the United States Navy into a power.

It was a herculean task, but not impossible; the North possessed an abundance of industry, raw materials and skilled workers. Under Welles's aegis, the Navy would increase its annual expenditures tenfold, topping $123 million by the War's end. And the wartime Navy would eventually boast 670 ships, 8,700 officers and 51,500 seamen.

Like Welles, his opposite number, Confederate Secretary of the Navy Stephen R. Mallory, had been appointed to give his state, Florida, representation in the Cabinet. Mallory, however, was far more familiar than Welles with naval affairs. As United States Senator he had been Chairman of the Naval Affairs Committee and probably knew more about nautical matters than any other Southern politician. He was progressive in matters of naval design and had expressed interest in the future of ironclad warships.

Mallory understood that if the blockade was to be broken, the Confederacy would have to challenge the U.S. Navy with a relatively small number of specialized ships. The privateers would help only if the neutral powers allowed them to shelter prizes in their ports, or if they could penetrate the blockade to sell their booty and reap their profits in Southern ports. Besides, the government could not for long entrust its main naval offensive to profit-making concerns.

To stand any chance of extended success, the Confederate government would have to buy, build and operate fast, well-armed raiders to haunt the world's commercial shipping lanes. These cruisers could pay their own way by capturing Yankee merchantmen and

Gideon Welles, Lincoln's Secretary of the Navy, was attacked by the Northern press for running an inefficient, out-of-date Navy Department. But insiders appreciated his modernization efforts. "The department," enthused a senior officer in June 1861, "has vitality and energy never seen there before."

Confederate Secretary of the Navy Stephen R. Mallory faced an odd problem early in the War: dozens of excess senior officers in a Navy of only 12 small ships. He solved it by relegating older officers to face-saving permanent rank in an inactive Regular Navy, and by placing men of fighting age in a Provisional Navy where they could earn promotions for meritorious service.

cargoes as prizes or, if that failed, by destroying the enemy ships. They might lure Yankee warships into vain pursuit, thereby thinning the blockade and making it easier for the runners to penetrate. And the Confederate Navy also needed ironclad ships and iron-prowed rams to drive off or sink Federal blockaders.

Since the Confederacy lacked the industrial facilities for shipbuilding, and since the required ships would take considerable time to build or to modify from existing craft, Mallory immediately sent agents to England to commission or buy the vessels. Mallory's agents also toured the South, acquiring miscellaneous ships to arm as coastal defenders. Besides the Federal revenue cutters seized in Southern ports, Navy agents and local authorities took over by purchase or confiscation any Northern-owned vessels that failed to escape after the start of hostilities.

There was a great outpouring of Southerners and Britishers eager to get into the blockade-running business. Entrepreneurs started establishing syndicates to finance large, transatlantic blockade-runners. But that would take time. Meanwhile, Bermuda and the Bahamas, respectively less than 650 and 150 miles off the Confederate coast, were natural transfer points for cargoes from Europe, and such voyages could be made easily and at once by many a competent mariner owning a small, seaworthy ship. Before long, scores of schooners, sloops and other coastal vessels put out from Southern ports for Nassau in the Bahamas and the port of St. George on Bermuda.

Like Mallory, Secretary Welles organized a massive effort to collect stopgap ships for blockade duty. He was much better funded, but he needed many more ships to supplement and support the Union warships that soon began returning from foreign stations and emerging from the shipyards of Philadelphia, Brooklyn and Boston. Welles and his aides decided that they must blockade 10 major Southern ports connected to the Confederate interior by railroads or navigable rivers. The targeted ports were: Norfolk, Virginia; New Bern, Beaufort and Wilmington in North Carolina; Charleston, South Carolina; Savannah, Georgia; Fernandina and Pensacola in Florida; Mobile, Alabama; and New Orleans, Louisiana.

To lead the ship-buying program, Welles sent his brother-in-law, Charles D. Morgan, to seaports throughout the North. Spending freely, Morgan leased or purchased just about anything big enough to be armed or sound enough to support the warships: cargo ships, coal barges, ferryboats, yachts, packet boats, tugboats. All were bought or chartered by the U.S. Navy and turned over to shipyards for quick modifications.

The work of refitting and arming the motley vessels to make them effective blockaders required a magician's touch and a marine engineer's skill. It was rather like "altering a vest into a shirt," observed Captain Samuel F. Du Pont, commandant of the Philadelphia Navy Yard. Nevertheless, some of the makeshift ships did yeoman service. The *Somerset*, a lowly ferryboat in former days, confronted and captured the sleek blockade-runner *Circassian*, one of the War's most valuable prizes. It was really quite easy. The *Circassian* tried to get away, but Lieutenant Earl English, captain of the *Somerset*, bracketed her with two shells and put another into her rigging. At that, the blockade-runner surrendered.

As this fleet of rented and refitted ships joined the existing Navy vessels on station off Southern ports, plans were being drafted and bids let for the new Union fleet built expressly for blockade duty. Here the North showed its industrial might, for the first of these vessels, the steam sloop *Tuscarora*, was launched at Philadelphia on the 22nd of August, 1861. Welles boasted, "Her keel was growing in the forests three months ago."

In quick succession there came 23 steam-powered gunboats, each displacing about 600 tons, armed with four to seven guns, and designed with shallow drafts to enable them to work close inshore. From keel-laying to commissioning, each was completed in about three months—hence the sobriquet "90-day gunboats." These were soon followed by a unique class of side-wheel double-enders designed for service on rivers and in narrow channels. Like ferryboats, they had two bows with a rudder at each end, enabling them to reverse direction in constricted waters without turning around. With a fair turn of speed, comparatively heavy armament and shallow drafts, they made excellent inshore blockaders.

Manning the growing Navy was an unremitting problem for Welles. He first had to replace the pro-Confederate Navy officers who "went South" and left critical gaps in the command structure. To help fill these holes, the Navy Department ordered to sea duty the three upper classes at its decade-old Naval Academy, which had been hastily moved from Annapolis to Newport, Rhode Island, when slave-owning Maryland briefly threatened to secede. Volunteer commissions—as opposed to Regular Navy commissions—were offered to promising men from all walks, particularly those with ex-

Stacks of cannonballs frame a laid-up steamer at Florida's Pensacola Navy Yard, seized from th

ederal authorities before the War. Other Confederate booty included 33 cannon, about 500 barrels of gunpowder and a large quantity of small-arms ammunition.

perience in the merchant fleet. Training courses were offered in the Navy yards, though they were so hurried and haphazard that many new officers arrived at their ships barely acquainted with their duties. Eventually the commissioned volunteers would outnumber Regular Navy officers by 4 to 1.

At first, enlisted men poured into the Navy. Thousands of these volunteers were foreigners—Irishmen predominating—and thousands more would come from the ranks of slaves freed by Army operations. But by 1863 the stream of volunteers had dwindled, and to add incentive an enlistment bonus was offered.

The blockade produced its first success just five days after Lincoln declared it. On April 24 the Federal sailing sloop *Cumberland*, together with a few small vessels she had enlisted, began seizing ships in the vicinity of Fort Monroe, Virginia. Within two weeks, the *Cumberland's* commander, Flag Officer (then the Navy's top rank) Garrett J. Pendergrast, had stopped or captured 16 ships. Other blockaders soon captured prizes. On the 12th of May off Charleston, the Federal steam frigate *Niagara* snapped up a Confederate merchantman homeward bound from Liverpool.

By the end of July, the addition of ships had made the blockading fleet large enough to be divided into three commands: the North Atlantic Squadron, covering the area from the Potomac to Cape Henry, North Carolina; the South Atlantic Squadron, extending southward to Key West; and the Gulf Squadron, responsible for the rest of the coast to the Mexican border. Union warships now patrolled the entrance to every major Southern port.

It was not enough. Nights were dark, the seas were wide and Southern pilots were expert at navigating among the numerous sounds, bays and inlets that dotted the shoreline. Ships ran the blockade with such ease and consistency that Southerners could well afford to mock the efforts of the United States Navy. "You have heard, no doubt, Old Abe has blockaded our port," a Charlestonian wrote to an English friend in May 1861. "A nice blockade indeed! On the second day, a British ship, the *A and A*, ran the gantlet with a snug freight of $30,000. Today two vessels passed safely in, both British, I understand. Don't you wish you had a hundred ships for one voyage?"

By September, large, specially built transatlantic blockade-runners were beginning to bring in important cargoes. Fraser, Trenholm & Company, a Southern shipping and banking firm with offices in Liverpool, sent over the *Bermuda*, which arrived in Savannah on September 28 with a big load of weapons and general supplies. Though Fraser, Trenholm profited handsomely by the shipment, the firm's purpose had been to demonstrate the inefficiency of the blockade. This the *Bermuda* accomplished easily, slipping into port without meeting a single blockader. The auspices for blockade-running were excellent, to say the least.

All the while, Confederate privateers were pressing the South's naval offensive. Within days of President Davis' offer of letters of marque, Southern entrepreneurs were forming syndicates to underwrite the costs of arming and manning whatever vessels could be found. By May 6, 1861, when the Confederate Congress ratified Davis' privateering proclamation, more than 3,000 applications had been submitted to state and Confeder-

The wooden side-wheeler U.S.S. *Morse*, carrying two 9-inch cannon, was one of many workaday vessels converted to warships. Built as a ferryboat for service in New York, she was hastily refitted as a Federal blockader in November 1861.

ate authorities. Raphael Semmes, who soon would win international celebrity as the captain of a Confederate Navy commerce raider, recognized the danger as well as the appeal of privateering. In a letter to a Confederate congressman, he wrote: "Private cupidity will always furnish the means for this description of warfare, and all that will be required of you will be to put it under sufficient legal restraints to prevent it from degenerating into piracy."

Like blockade-running, privateering began quickly and with resounding success. The first Confederate privateer to venture into the Gulf of Mexico was merely a converted towboat, but she bore an elegant Southern name, the *Calhoun*, and she did it honor. Before she was 24 hours out of New Orleans, the little five-gun steamer captured a Yankee bark carrying 3,100 barrels of lime, and within 48 hours she had taken two more Union merchantmen.

The *Calhoun* was soon joined at sea by other New Orleans ships whose owners were eager to cash in on the easy pickings. On May 26, however, the U.S.S. *Brooklyn* took up her blockading station at the passes of the Mississippi. A formidable 25-gun steam sloop, the *Brooklyn* blocked the port of New Orleans to all but speedy, shallow-draft blockade-runners. The privateers and their prize ships, built with deep drafts for stability on ocean voyages and thereby excluded from the chief local market, gradually shifted their operations out of the Gulf of Mexico.

Charleston, currently receiving less attention from the blockaders than New Orleans, became the hub of Confederate privateering.

The Stone Fleets: An Exercise in Futility

In June of 1861, a top-level naval-strategy board in Washington advised the Navy Department that the easiest way to tighten the Union blockade was to buy some useless old ships, load them with stones and sink them to close the entrances to Southern harbors. The idea was as old as blockading itself, but executing it led to a long and distressing comedy of errors.

In July, 22 schooners that once hauled coal, cotton and wood were loaded with rock; orders were issued to sink them in vital inlets off the North Carolina coast. But after the so-called stone fleet had been towed from Baltimore to Hampton Roads, Virginia, Flag Officer Silas H. Stringham of the Atlantic Blockading Squadron decided the scheme was a waste of time and manpower. He detained 20 of the ships and gave the other two to General Benjamin Butler to use as supply vessels for an upcoming attack on the Confederate forts at Hatteras Inlet.

In September, when Captain Louis Goldsborough relieved Stringham as flag officer of the squadron, his superiors immediately began badgering him to carry out the original order. But, to the Navy Department's embarrassment, only three of the original 22 schooners were still afloat; the others had sprung leaks and sunk in Hampton Roads. Finally, in November, Goldsborough reported with great relief that the survivors had been sunk as directed.

But that was not the end of it. Washington was preparing a grander stone fleet of 45 ships, most of them blunt-nosed, square-sterned New England whalers. Their target: Savannah, Georgia. The whalers actually arrived before Savannah on November 25, but the Federals discovered that the job had already been done for them. The Confederates, mistaking the whalers for an invasion fleet,

had sunk three steamers across the harbor's entrance to keep the Yankees out.

So the Federals hauled their stone fleet to another port, Charleston. In late December, 16 whalers were sunk in the harbor's main channel (*below*). A month later, 13 more were sunk in a secondary channel.

Meanwhile, squawks of protest came from the Confederacy's trading partners. Great Britain and France denounced the mass sinkings as "monstrously unfair" and "indefensibly barbaric." Secretary of State William H. Seward repeatedly assured the Europeans that the United States would remove the obstacles after the War.

But greater forces were settling the issue. The tides and currents were at work, and in just four months new channels had been scoured out. Charleston Harbor was open once more, and the blockade-runners were back in business.

A group of whaling captains, hired by the United States Navy, confer before boarding their rock-filled vessels for the trip south. Mercifully, the captains of the stone fleet were not asked to scuttle their own ships. "The only service required of you," stated the orders, "is the safe delivery of your vessel."

A U.S. Navy task force sinks a fleet of New England whalers, some of them laden with more than 500 tons of rock, across the bar of Charleston's main ship channel on December 20, 1861. The vessels were positioned in a checkerboard pattern for maximum efficiency as obstacles.

But here too the life of a privateer was precarious, as the crew of the schooner *Savannah* found out. The ship, captained by one Thomas Baker and armed with an 18-pound swivel gun dating from the War of 1812, put to sea on June 3. The next day she captured a brig laden with sugar and sent her into Georgetown, South Carolina, with a prize crew. But immediately the *Savannah's* luck ran out. As her crewmen celebrated their easy victory, a lookout sighted a sail in the distance. Closing on the new quarry, Captain Baker discovered too late that she was no merchant ship but the U.S. Navy brig *Perry*.

As the *Perry* opened her gunports and ran out her guns, the *Savannah* began frantic maneuvers to escape. But Yankee shots panicked the *Savannah's* crew, making flight impossible and forcing Baker to strike his colors. A Union prize crew boarded the Confederate ship, whose 20 officers and men were the first privateers to be captured by the North. They were taken to New York City and, as Lincoln had threatened, were charged with piracy.

The stage was set for a grim test of wills between Abraham Lincoln and Jefferson Davis. During the trial, Davis answered Lincoln's threat with a letter warning that the Confederate government would "deal out to the prisoners held by it the same treatment and the same fate as shall be experienced by those captured on the *Savannah*." True to his warning, 13 of the highest ranking Union officers in Confederate custody were chosen by lot to be executed if the Southern seamen in New York suffered that fate. Fortunately for all concerned, the New York jury was unable to reach a verdict.

Before a new trial could commence, the execution issue shifted to William W. Smith of the *Jefferson Davis*, a former slave ship that was now a privateer out of Charleston. Evading the blockade, the privateer had put to sea on June 28, 1861. She took several prizes, including a schooner named the *Enchantress*. All of the *Enchantress'* crewmen, except for the black cook, Jacob Garrick, were taken off, and Smith was sent aboard in charge of a prize crew.

The *Enchantress* was headed for Charleston when she was spied and overtaken by the *Albatross*, a U.S. Navy steamer. On being hailed by an officer aboard the *Albatross*, Smith correctly identified his ship, then answered the question "Where bound?" with a reasonable lie: "Santiago de Cuba." At this point, Garrick the cook broke free and ran up on deck shouting that the *Enchantress* was a Confederate prize. He leaped overboard and was rescued by the *Albatross*. Smith and his crew were made prisoners.

Smith was tried for piracy, convicted, and sentenced to death. But Federal officials decided that the Confederate government intended to carry out its threat of retaliation for any executed privateers. They quietly transferred Smith from his death cell in a New York jail to a prisoner-of-war camp.

Thereafter, all captured privateers were treated as war prisoners; none were hanged, and so no retaliatory executions took place. Jefferson Davis had won his battle of nerves with Abraham Lincoln, and for Davis it was a prestige-raising victory. Practically no one praised Lincoln for humanely backing down, saving lives that would have been squandered in tit-for-tat executions.

Privateers outdid themselves in the summer of 1861, boldly searching for prey off New York City and Boston. As Northern fears mounted, Gideon Welles came under

A U.S. Navy poster urges men to enlist for one year as a sure means of avoiding conscription (which lasted until the War's end). The broadside also promised a share of prize monies from captured Confederate vessels. Actually, all the prizes captured yielded less than one third of the sum claimed in the poster.

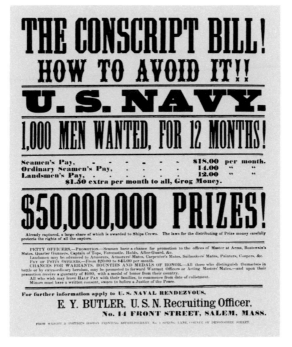

THE CONSCRIPT BILL!
HOW TO AVOID IT!!
U. S. NAVY.
1,000 MEN WANTED, FOR 12 MONTHS!

Seamen's Pay, - - - - - - $18.00 per month.
Ordinary Seamen's Pay, - - - - 14.00 " "
Landsmen's Pay, - - - - - 12.00 " "
$1.50 extra per month to all, Grog Money.

$50,000,000 PRIZES!

Already captured, a large share of which is awarded to Ships Crews. The laws for the distributing of Prize money carefully protects the rights of all the captors.

PETTY OFFICERS,—PROMOTION.—Seamen have chance for promotion to the offices of Master at Arms, Boatswain's Mates, Quarter Gunners, Captain of Tops, Forecastle, Holds, After-Guard, &c.
Landsmen may be advanced to Armorers, Armorers' Mates, Carpenter's Mates, Sailmakers' Mates, Painters, Coopers, &c.
PAY OF PETTY OFFICERS,—From $20.00 to $45.00 per month.
CHANCES FOR WARRANTS, BOUNTIES AND MEDALS OF HONOR.—All those who distinguish themselves in battle or by extraordinary heroism, may be promoted to forward Warrant Officers or Acting Masters' Mates,—and upon their promotion receive a guaranty of $100, with a medal of honor from their country.
All who may leave HALF PAY with their families, to commence from date of enlistment.
Minors must have a written consent, sworn to before a Justice of the Peace.

For further information apply to U. S. NAVAL RENDEZVOUS,
E. Y. BUTLER, U. S. N. Recruiting Officer,
No. 14 FRONT STREET, SALEM, MASS.

FROM WRIGHT & POTTER'S BOSTON PRINTING ESTABLISHMENT, No. 1 SPRING LANE, CORNER OF DEVONSHIRE STREET.

intense pressure from shipping interests and mayors of coastal towns, who begged and demanded that he divert ships from blockade duty to hunt down the so-called pirates. Welles's decision to concentrate the Navy's resources on the blockade was denounced as pure madness, and the Secretary was described as a man possessed, a Rip Van Winkle snoozing while the nation's seaborne trade expired. Welles, certain that privateering would stop when the Southern ports were shut tight, ignored the protests.

Welles continued to strengthen the blockade in every way he could. He realized that the blockade was weakened regularly and for long periods whenever a Federal ship off the coast of South Carolina, Florida or the Gulf states had to steam all the way back to the nearest Union-held base, Hampton Roads, for fuel, food and ammunition. The U.S. Navy base at Key West had also remained in Union hands, but its facilities were inad-

equate. Welles concluded that good, strategic Southern coastal points must be captured and turned into coaling stations and supply bases for the blockading ships.

Toward this end, a joint naval-military commission known as the Blockade Strategy Board met under Captain Samuel F. Du Pont in June 1861. The targets chosen for joint Army-Navy assaults were Port Royal Sound between Charleston and Savannah, and Ship Island, off Biloxi, Mississippi. In addition, the board decided that Hatteras Inlet, leading to Pamlico Sound and thence to the chief North Carolina ports, must be closed to blockade-runners and opened to future Union assaults. These attacks, fundamentally logistical operations for the Navy, differed from a number of much-larger landings whose ultimate purpose was military operations against Confederate ports.

The first of the base-capturing attacks began on the morning of August 28, 1861. Some 900 Union soldiers under Major General Benjamin F. Butler put out in small boats from two offshore transports and tried to land on the beach near Hatteras Inlet. At the same time, three warships led by Flag Officer Silas H. Stringham opened fire on Forts Clark and Hatteras, the two log-and-sand strong points guarding the inlet.

It was a windy morning, and the landing boats capsized in the foaming surf. Only the first wave, 319 men, made it ashore; they could not fight because their gunpowder was wet and useless, and the loss of their boats meant that the rest of the soldiers could not be landed. But the warships were doing much better, thanks to a new tactic Stringham adopted. Instead of bombarding the forts from an anchored position, as sail-driven warships commonly did to neutralize

the vagaries of wind and tide, Stringham ordered his vessels to fire steadily while on the move. Thus they presented elusive targets to the Confederate gunners and forced them to change their range constantly.

The Confederates fought back gamely, but their guns lacked the range of the Federal cannon and their ammunition was in short supply. It was a one-sided battle. Just after midday, Fort Clark ran out of shells and its garrison fled to Fort Hatteras. While General Butler's troops occupied the abandoned installation, the ships focused their fire on the remaining strong point, pouring shells into the fort at the rate of as many as 28 per minute. The hapless Confederates took cover in a bombproof shelter; early the next morning they raised the white flag.

About two weeks later, Union soldiers walked ashore at Ship Island, Mississippi, which had been abandoned by the Confederates. The island gave them a base from which they could patrol the entrances to both the Mississippi River and Mobile Bay. Now only one of the primary targets remained.

After Charleston, Port Royal was the Confederacy's best natural harbor on the Atlantic, and the Union prepared elaborately for its capture. At Hampton Roads, Flag Officer Du Pont amassed a fleet of 17 warships, 25 supply vessels and 25 transports to carry the expeditionary force of 12,000 soldiers under Brigadier General Thomas W. Sherman. The flotilla set sail in late October, but it ran into a storm off Cape Hatteras that claimed three vessels and scattered the rest. The ships limped to the rendezvous point off Port Royal, reorganized, and on November 7 launched the attack.

Two forts, Walker and Beauregard, stood on the headlands flanking the two-mile-wide entrance to the sound. Du Pont decided to attack them both at once. Borrowing a tactic from Flag Officer Stringham, he ordered his ships to sail in a long, oval course. Thus, in traveling each circuit, every ship brought her bow, broadside and stern guns to bear on one fort, then the other. The fleet's 155 guns rained shells on the Confederate redoubts "as fast," a Union officer said, "as a horse's feet beat the ground in a gallop."

The bombardment overwhelmed both of the Confederate garrisons, which had only 43 guns between them. During the afternoon the unnerved defenders abandoned their strong points and withdrew inland, leaving their guns intact and their personal belongings strewn along their line of retreat.

The seizure of Port Royal Sound gave the Federals a port in perfect operating condition (*pages 34-45*). Now great new swatches of Confederate coastline lay within range of Federal gunboat patrols. And supplies ferried from Port Royal to the blockading ships, or picked up by the blockaders on short trips to Port Royal, greatly increased the time that the warships could spend in the waters off Confederate ports.

For all practical purposes, the tightening of the blockade by various means put the privateers out of business by the end of 1861. The privateers with their deep-draft prizes could not penetrate the blockade, as shallow-draft blockade-runners did. And the privateers were also denied entry to foreign ports as other nations followed Britain's lead and declared neutrality. With so few ports open for the sale of prizes—and with so much risk for doubtful profits—privateers switched over in droves to the more lucrative business of blockade-running.

The quick demise of the privateers came

31

Confederate soldiers in Fort Walker trade
cannon fire with Federal warships circling in Port
Royal Sound. Among the warships was the U.S.S.
Pocahontas, whose captain, Commander Percival
Drayton, was the brother of the Confederate
commander, Brigadier General Thomas F. Drayton.

as no great loss to the Confederacy; they had served well as a stopgap for the Confederate Navy's commerce raiders, which began their destructive operations in the autumn of 1861. The privateers did have one lasting effect. The threat they posed to Union commerce panicked Northern shipping concerns and maritime insurance firms. Goods shipments were shifted to foreign vessels, and American merchantmen took shelter under the flags of neutral countries. The mighty American merchant fleet had begun a long retreat that the commerce raiders would soon turn into a rout.

On balance, the U.S. Navy had made more progress in 1861 than the Confederate Navy. More than 200 ships of various kinds had been added to the fleet, and the blockading force had grown so large that it was now divided for greater efficiency into four squadrons, two in the Gulf as well as the two in the Atlantic. And the Navy had increased by more than 15,000 officers and enlisted men, bringing its total strength to 24,000. President Lincoln passed a fair judgment on these developments in a report to Congress on December 3: "It may almost be said that a navy has been created and brought into service since our difficulties commenced."

Still, the U.S. Navy had a bigger job to do than the Confederate Navy, and its important gains gave no sign of becoming a decisive edge. One estimate held that as many as nine out of every 10 blockade-runners had reached Southern ports safely in 1861. And though the war at sea had stabilized during the year of improvisations, there was no telling how the pattern would be disrupted by those bizarre new ships about to make their American debut: the ironclads.

A Union Foothold in the Old South

After Flag Officer Samuel F. Du Pont and his 17 United States warships drove the Confederates out of Forts Walker and Beauregard in November of 1861, twelve thousand U.S. soldiers occupied the islands of Port Royal Sound, South Carolina. Port Royal fast became a coaling station, supply depot and repair shop for blockading ships. The strategic island of Hilton Head soon harbored a bustling Yankee community with its own hospital, church, printing office, bakery and theater, as well as a long line of shanties known as Robber's Row, where anything from hoop skirts to pocket watches could be had at exorbitant prices.

"Here we are," a soldier happily wrote home, "surrounded by cotton, sweet potatoes, corn, beans, mules, oranges, palmetto trees, Southern pines, niggers, palm and peanuts." The area did have its drawbacks for the soldiers and sailors stationed there. Mosquitoes from the swampy lowlands carried malaria and yellow fever, and summer temperatures of 110° F. were common.

The heat was relieved, however, by sea breezes and plentiful shade trees, and life was slow and easy. Officers were served by freed slaves who regarded them as liberators and gladly accepted small wages. Infantrymen of the 3rd New Hampshire Regiment found a plantation with an immense blackberry field; they ate their fill and made wine of the rest. Sailors and soldiers harvested brierwood roots in the swamps and carved fanciful pipes. Little wonder that a Yankee who served at Port Royal called it "the sunny side of the soldier's life."

Federal soldiers guard the waterfront battlements of South Carolina's Fort Walker, which was later renamed Fort Welles after Lincoln's Secretary of the Navy. The guns, left behind by the fleeing Confederates, remain trained on Port Royal Sound, where U.S. Navy warships and transport vessels ride peacefully at anchor.

At the abandoned plantation of John E. Seabrook on Edisto Island, former slaves tend cotton that has been spread out to dry after being seized from a blockade-runner.

The Hilton Head home of General Thomas F. Drayton, former commander at Port Royal, is occupied by bluecoats and some former slave women. The general's brother, Captain Percival Drayton, chose to fight for the Union; he captained one of the attacking ships that drove General Drayton from his command and his home.

Many blacks, jubilant at the arrival of the Federals, took over their former masters' houses and continued working the plantations.

At Hilton Head, a Federal commissary and officers' quarters stand beside a pier, where light craft unload men and supplies from the larger vessels anchored far out in the bay. The lumber used in building the Hilton Head installations came from the island's magnificent pine trees, some of them 100 feet tall.

A corpsman signals to a ship at sea from a platform overlooking the bay at Hilton Head. Signaled messages were spelled out in two simple flag movements, made in differing combinations and repetitions for each letter of the alphabet.

The main signal station at Hilton Head was a former plantation house with a rooftop tower added to extend its signaling range. Through this station uncounted messages passed between the warships at sea and nearby Federal Army headquarters.

On Otter Island, a corpsman signals from the top of a 142-foot tower encircled by a stockade for defense against enemy attack. Seven such towers were built at intervals between Hilton Head and Folly Island, 55 miles to the north, and a message could be relayed from one end of the line to the other within minutes.

A prime product of Yankee ingenuity, this floating repair shop—shown in a retouched photo—was formed by lashing together two old whaling vessels, roofing them over and fitting them out with a brass foundry and a smithy. The structure also housed tin, pattern and boiler shops along with living quarters for the workmen.

In a dockside building, a lar[ge] condenser purified sea water [for] use in powering the blockad[ing] steamships. Untreated salt wa[ter] would have fouled the ships' boile[rs]

The United States Naval Foundry at Port Royal forged the replacement parts needed by ironclads arriving for repairs.

On the deck of the U.S. monitor *Passaic*, the captain acts as chaplain during a Sunday morning service for Federal sailors. To provide a patriotic touch, the U.S. flag has been draped over the makeshift altar.

Off-duty Union infantrymen lounge about in a rowboat under the warm Carolina sun. Beyond them, in the broad bay between Morris Island and Hilton Head, lie

44

e paddle-wheeler *Commodore McDonough*, a former New York ferry that had been converted into a blockade gunboat.

Encounter at Hampton Roads

*"I regard the possession of an iron-armored ship as a matter of the first necessity.
Such a vessel at this time could traverse the entire coast of the United States, prevent
all blockades, and encounter, with a fair prospect of success, their entire Navy."*

STEPHEN R. MALLORY, CONFEDERATE SECRETARY OF THE NAVY, MAY 8, 1861

March 8, 1862, started out as just another day of waiting for the 2,000-odd Federal seamen on board the 17 ships of the fast-growing North Atlantic Blockading Squadron. Their assignment was to hold Hampton Roads, a wide, shallow channel eight miles long where three Virginia rivers join and flow into the Chesapeake Bay. This strategic waterway was vital to both sides, but the situation there had been stalemated for 10 months. The Federal warships had made no serious effort to defeat the Confederate gunboats and shore defenses in the James River, which prevented them from sailing upriver to Richmond, about 100 miles to the northwest. And the James River gunboats were not strong enough to challenge the Federal blockaders for control of Hampton Roads and access to the sea.

The land forces surrounding Hampton Roads were deadlocked as well. Confederate troops held the southern bank, including Portsmouth and Norfolk, the Gosport Navy Yard and a ring of shore batteries stretching from the mouth of the James and Nansemond Rivers to Sewell's Point and the mouth of the Elizabeth River. A Federal force held the northern bank; it had never lost control of Fort Monroe and from there it had taken over the towns of Newport News and Hampton by the previous July.

The Federal sailors in Hampton Roads expected no trouble that March 8. To be sure, they had heard tales about a mighty Confederate ironclad ship; she was being constructed nearby from the ruins of the U.S.S. *Merrimac*, and for months it had been rumored that she would soon come to slaughter them like sheep. The rumors had caused consternation in Washington and had pushed the Navy Department to begin its own ironclad-building program with an odd little experimental craft called the *Monitor*. But the *Merrimac* did not appear, and the Yankee sailors, having heard "Wolf!" cried so many times, figured she never would. It was quite enough to make bored men cranky. "We have nothing new here," wrote Captain Henry Van Brunt from his steam frigate *Minnesota*. "All is quiet. The *Merrimac* is still invisible to us, but report says she is ready to come out. I sincerely wish she would; I am quite tired of hearing of her."

Shortly after noon, a lookout on the Federal gunboat *Zouave* spotted a curl of black smoke on the horizon in the Confederate-controlled Elizabeth River. The *Zouave's* skipper, Henry Reaney, got permission to reconnoiter and chugged two miles into the channel. Then, recalled Reaney, "We saw what looked like the roof of a very big barn belching smoke as from a chimney on fire. We were all divided in opinion as to what was coming. The bosun's mate was the first to make out the Confederate flag, and then we all guessed it was the *Merrimac* come at last."

Reaney ordered his crew to quarters and fired six shots from his single gun, a Parrott 30-pounder. The shots bounced harmlessly off the sides of the awful iron monster, which

John Ericsson, the imperious Swedish-born engineer, dominated naval architecture of the Civil War. While building the *Monitor* for the U.S. Navy, he dashed off at least 20 patentable inventions—from a four-fluke anchor to a flush toilet that worked below the ship's water line.

was bearing down relentlessly on the *Cumberland*, a 24-gun sailing sloop.

Thus began 24 hours of epic naval action. First, the *Merrimac* would prove conclusively what naval architects and the admiralties of the European powers firmly believed but had never fully tested: that wooden ships were doomed in battles with iron vessels. And then would come the climactic clash between the two ironclads. Northerners and Southerners alike, believing that the sea war might well turn on this struggle, waited anxiously to learn the winner.

The *Merrimac* combined several threads in a revolution that had been transforming naval architecture since Robert Fulton designed the first commercially successful steamboat in 1807. As steamships were improved, they won limited favor among merchant shipowners, but aroused little interest among the major navies of the world. Except for tugs and dispatch vessels, the navies built no steam-driven vessels for nearly 25 years.

To the admirals and architects who decided naval design, steam created more problems than it solved. Engines and boilers took up space needed to store ammunition and supplies, and they were extremely vulnerable to enemy gunfire. To complicate matters further, the early steamships were propelled by cumbersome paddle wheels that were easy targets and that preempted space formerly allocated to guns. And finally, the early steam engines were inefficient. Their low boiler pressures limited ship speed to a few knots, and they consumed fuel so fast that, unless frequent refueling stops were made, the engines could be run only selectively. Steamships spent most of their time under sail, using steam primarily to travel against the wind or to maneuver in a harbor.

A radical advance came in 1836; independently, the English inventor Francis Pettit-Smith and the Swedish engineer John Ericsson developed a screw propeller that made steam engines practical for warships. Screw propellers were considerably more powerful and efficient than paddle wheels. They also allowed the placement of engines and boilers below the water line, where they were shielded from enemy gunfire.

Indeed, added protection for the whole ship became increasingly essential toward 1850 with the great strides made in ordnance technology. Solid shot was being replaced by explosive shells, which could blow apart the sturdiest wooden vessels. And the old smoothbore cannon were being supplemented by guns whose rifled bores gave them much longer range and greater accuracy.

Because of the new weaponry, iron plating became an important feature of warship design. The early experiments with sheet armor were primitive affairs. But during the Crimean War, the French used three ironclad floating batteries to force the surrender of a Russian Black Sea fortress near Odessa.

After the Crimean War, recent naval innovations were brought together in the French ironclad wooden steam frigate *Gloire* and the British steam frigate *Warrior*, one of the first iron-hulled, armored warships. Soon every major European power built warships patterned after them. But no one had an opportunity to test ironclad against ironclad—until the American Civil War broke out.

The ironclad's evolution was of course well known to Confederate Navy Secretary Stephen R. Mallory, who had kept abreast of changing naval and ordnance technology as the prewar Chairman of the United States Senate's Naval Affairs Committee. Mallory knew that the hidebound U.S. Navy had been slow to follow the trend from the old technology to the new. The most modern Federal warships were transitional craft propelled by both sail and steam, but they were basically little changed from the men-of-war sailed by Sir Francis Drake some 250 years earlier. Mallory reasoned that if the infant Confederate Navy was to compete at sea with the much larger Federal Navy, he must step boldly into the future.

On May 8, he presented his plan for building ironclads to the Confederate Committee on Naval Affairs. The venture would be costly but worth the price, he argued, for the ironclads' invulnerability would cancel the U.S. Navy's enormous advantage in numbers. "Not a moment should be lost," he urged. The committee granted him two million dollars to proceed with his plans.

Formidable obstacles stood in Mallory's path. Technicians of all kinds were in short supply. Not a single shipyard in the South was able to build even a small warship from scratch. Only one Southern rolling mill, the Tredegar Iron Works in Richmond, could produce sheet iron, and it was already overloaded with orders from the Army and the railroads—orders that seemed far more important than Mallory's.

For help, Mallory turned to three imaginative Southerners: fellow Floridian John Brooke, an ordnance expert; William Williamson, a naval engineer; and John Porter, a naval builder. Porter had been involved with ironclads; in 1846, he had tried to interest the U.S. Navy in one of his own designs. He would use features of this original design to convert the *Merrimac*.

The *Merrimac*, which had been scuttled and burned by the Federals when they evacuated the Gosport Navy Yard in April 1861, turned out to be a salvageable wreck. On May 30, 1861, the charred hulk was raised from the shallows of the Elizabeth River and put in dry dock. The hull was razeed—cut away to the top of the 17½-foot screw propeller, exposing the tops of the engines and steam boilers. These well-worn parts had been scheduled for replacement by the U.S. Navy, and 40 days submerged in the Elizabeth River had done nothing to improve them. But engines and boilers, regardless of their condition, were priceless items to the Confederates. Williamson set to work overhauling the *Merrimac's* machinery.

One design problem could not be solved: The wooden frigate had been built with a deep draft, 22 feet, for stability in high-seas duty. Since the ironclad would draw the same 22 feet of water, she would have to maneuver carefully in local operations: The central channel of the Elizabeth River was only 24 feet deep, and Hampton Roads was seamed with tricky shoals.

Once Williamson had rehabilitated the machinery, Porter covered it with a new gun deck. In turn he covered that deck with a fortlike casemate that was framed with 20-inch pine timbers, planked with four inches of oak and plated with two layers of sheet iron, each two inches thick. The casemate's sides were slanted at an angle of 35 degrees to cause enemy shells to glance off. The iron sides were designed to extend two feet below the water line to protect against ramming and near-misses.

The casemate housed 10 big guns: one 7-inch pivot gun at the bow, another at the stern, and three 9-inch smoothbore Dahlgrens and one 6-inch rifled cannon on each broadside. Brooke made rifled cannon out of old-fashioned smoothbores, cutting spiral grooves into the bores and then putting red-hot iron bands over the powder chambers to shrink while cooling, thus reinforcing the barrels against the increased firing pressures. For her final weapon, the *Merrimac* was equipped with a massive 1,500-pound cast-iron prow for ramming enemy ships.

By now the Confederates were well aware that the *Monitor* was a-building, and they tried to speed up the completion of their ship. But their efforts were thwarted by delays at the Tredegar foundry. Brooke spent much of his time badgering production officials there—to little avail. It took Tredegar until February—three months after the scheduled launching—to turn out the 723 tons of armor plating that were required.

On February 17, 1862, after almost nine months of labor, the ship was commissioned and launched as the C.S.S. *Virginia.* Southerners usually called her that. But to her Yankee foes and in later tradition, she continued to be known as the *Merrimac.* Actually, the ship's name was originally spelled *Merrimack,* but the *k* had been dropped in common usage.

The task of recruiting a crew was a difficult one. Finding enough officers was not the problem; several hundred U.S. Navy officers had resigned their commissions and joined the Confederacy, so it was relatively easy to round up the required complement of 30 vigorous and experienced young men. But the 300 sailors needed were hard to find; many qualified Southern seamen, discouraged by the small size of the Confederate Navy, had joined the Army instead, or were working aboard blockade-runners. Mallory asked Lieutenant John Taylor Wood, an experienced Navy officer and the brother-in-law of President Jefferson Davis, to scour the Confederate Army camps at Yorktown, Richmond and Petersburg for men with some knowledge of the sea, or at least with some artillery experience. Wood managed to persuade the Army to release some sailors.

Mallory created a new post, commander of the James River defenses and therefore the *Merrimac,* and he chose old Commodore Franklin Buchanan to serve as flag officer. Buchanan had been one of the most distinguished officers of the U.S. Navy. Among the highlights of his 46 years of service, he had organized the Naval Academy at Annapolis in 1845. Buchanan reported to Gosport on February 25, 1862.

Coal, powder and supplies were now carried aboard the *Merrimac.* Someone had discovered a critical shortage of flannel, used to make gunpowder bags. With the aid of the local newspaper, a story was published urging patriotic women to contribute their flannel dresses and skirts. Flannel aplenty was contributed. By March 7 the last batch of powder had been brought aboard, and the *Merrimac* was ready for action.

Meanwhile, the U.S. Navy got off to a late start in ironclad building. Navy Secretary Gideon Welles, preoccupied with acquiring ships to blockade the Southern ports, soon learned that the *Merrimac* was being converted, but he was slow to recognize the threat she would pose to Union shipping.

At a Naval Affairs Committee meeting in May 1861, Welles had broached the idea of buying or building ironclads. But the subject was tabled until July, when he recommended to Congress that a board of ironclad experts be convened.

Another month dragged by before Welles

The U.S. Navy's *Merrimac (left)*, a 40-gun, three-masted steam frigate, burns at the Gosport Navy Yard near Norfolk, Virginia, after being scuttled by retreating Union forces in April of 1862. Nine months later, after extensive remodeling by the Confederate Navy, the ship emerged as a giant ironclad *(below)*.

received the authority and the funds to establish his advisory board. He chose three distinguished Navy men: Commodore Hiram Paulding, Commodore Joseph Smith and Commander Charles H. Davis. The conservative old salts began their deliberations in mid-August with a timid disclaimer, announcing that they approached ironclads "with diffidence, having no experience, and but scanty knowledge in this branch of naval architecture."

The board members advertised for ironclad designs in Northern newspapers. Of the 17 that they received, they settled on two: a steam frigate, the *New Ironsides*, proposed by Merrick & Sons of Philadelphia, and an ironclad gunboat, called the *Galena*, designed by Cornelius Bushnell & Company of New Haven. But the Ironclad Board showed little enthusiasm for either.

Luckily for the Union, Bushnell was a patriot who wanted the best ship for his country. To begin with, he had his plans for the *Galena* appraised by John Ericsson, the eccentric Swedish-born inventor who in 1842 had designed the *Princeton*, the first American warship driven by a screw propeller.

It happened that Ericsson was currently at odds with the U.S. Navy, which had unfairly blamed him for a terrible accident almost 20 years before on board his *Princeton*. He had installed in the ship two 12-inch guns, one of his own design and the other, called "the Peacemaker," bored and finished under his personal direction. During a gunnery display on the Potomac River on the *Princeton's* second trial trip in 1844, the Peacemaker exploded, killing six people—including two members of President John Tyler's Cabinet. Though no charges were brought against Ericsson, the Navy refused to pay him for his work. Embittered, he vowed never to set foot in Washington again.

Bushnell took the plans for his ironclad to Ericsson's home in New York City. The engineer studied the plans and assured Bushnell that the *Galena* would work. Then he asked Bushnell to examine a plan of his own. Reaching into a dusty cupboard, Ericsson pulled out a cardboard model of a strange-looking, low, turreted vessel and explained how quickly and economically it could be built. Ericsson had sent a letter describing the vessel to Welles's Ironclad Board, but had received no answer.

Bushnell was immediately convinced that Ericsson's plan was superior to his own. He visited Welles to lobby for Ericsson's ship. He persuaded two influential New York iron manufacturers to intervene for him with Secretary of State William H. Seward, the former Governor of New York. To oblige them, Seward gave Bushnell a letter of introduction to President Lincoln.

When the Ironclad Board was called into special session on September 13 to hear Bushnell's presentation, the President himself appeared. Bushnell set forth his case well enough, but the board could not make up its mind. "All were surprised at the novelty of the plan," Bushnell recalled. "Some advised trying it; others ridiculed it." President Lincoln listened to the experts bicker back and forth and finally remarked: "All I have to say is what the girl said when she put her foot into the stocking: 'It strikes me there's something in it.' "

The President's folksy endorsement did not decide the matter. The board debated all the next day, then turned against Ericsson's design in the next morning's session.

It took hours of argument, but Bushnell

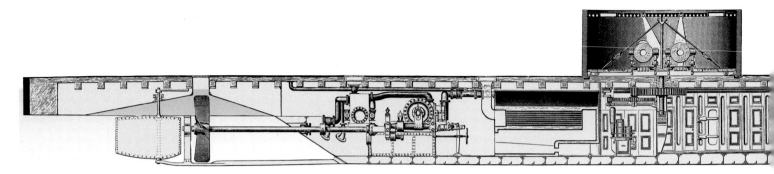

eventually won over Commodores Smith and Paulding. They insisted, however, that the board's decision must be unanimous, and Commander Davis did not want any part of an Ericsson-designed ship. Davis, glaring at Ericsson's cardboard model of the ship, angrily told Bushnell, "Take the little thing home and worship it, as it would not be idolatry, because it was made in the image of nothing in the heaven above or on the earth below or in the waters under the earth."

Exhausted, frustrated and thoroughly depressed, Bushnell could think of only one way to salvage the project. Somehow he had to get Ericsson—a forceful speaker whom Bushnell described as "a full electric battery in himself"—to break his vow and come to Washington to appear before the board.

Bushnell caught a train for New York, and the next morning he appeared on Ericsson's doorstep. Ericsson eagerly asked about the board's reaction. Bushnell, prepared to play on Ericsson's vanity, described the favorable reactions of Smith and Paulding and then paused significantly.

"How about Davis?" Ericsson asked.

"Oh, Davis," said Bushnell with all the nonchalance he could muster. "He wanted two or three explanations in detail which I couldn't give him, and so Secretary Welles proposed that I should get you to come to Washington and explain these few points to the entire board."

Ericsson declared, "I'll go tonight!"

So far so good. But the next afternoon when Ericsson showed up at the Navy Department, he discovered the truth. Not only was he an unexpected guest, he was an unwanted one too. The board told him flatly that his plan had been rejected and that there was no purpose in his visit.

Ericsson was outraged and nearly stormed from the room. But his pride got the better of his temper. Why, he wanted to know, had the board rejected his design?

Lack of stability, Smith replied.

This was too much for the engineer. Ericsson launched into a dazzling lecture on the physical principles that cause a ship to float, followed by a description of what his boat could do. For nearly one hour he held the board spellbound. "Gentlemen," he concluded, "I consider it to be your duty to the country to give me an order to build the vessel before I leave this room."

Gideon Welles, awaiting his board's final recommendation, asked Ericsson how long it would take and how much it would cost. Ericsson replied that he could build the ironclad in just 90 days for $275,000. That clinched it: Ericsson had won over the stubborn Commander Davis. The board, now unanimous, was so impressed it even extended his building time to 100 days. Welles urged Ericsson to begin work at once.

Returning to New York, Ericsson flung himself into the project. He made more than 100 detailed drawings of the ship and fed them to factories that would fabricate the parts and to an expert construction crew

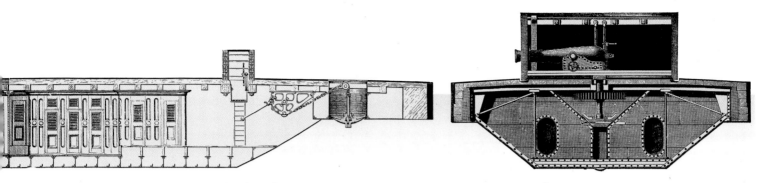

Ericsson's historic plan for the U.S.S. *Monitor* (*shown above in cross section*) featured a low silhouette that gave enemy gunners only two clear targets—a two-gun revolving turret amidships (*left*) and a cubical pilot house near the bow, where the captain and helmsman controlled the ship. The plan was based on a design that Ericsson had offered unsuccessfully to Napoleon III in 1854 to help France defeat Russia in the Crimean War.

at the Continental Iron Works in Brooklyn.

Ericsson's ship—he named her the *Monitor*—differed radically from the much-larger *Merrimac*. She was only 172 feet long and 41 feet 6 inches wide. Her hull was made of iron and was flat-bottomed; she sat in the water like a raft and looked like one, having only 18 inches of freeboard. Her draft would be barely half that of the *Merrimac*, just 10 feet 6 inches—ideal for shallow Southern coastal waters and for rivers with their snags and sand bars. On top of the hull was a flat wooden deck covered with two layers of half-inch iron plates. Armor hung over the sides like an iron skirt to protect against ramming and hits at the water line.

Slightly off-center on the ship's deck was her most original feature: a cylindrical revolving turret nine feet high with an inside diameter of 20 feet. The turret was fortified with eight layers of iron plating, each of them one inch thick. Turned by a small steam engine, the turret rested in a grooved bronze ring set into the deck. The turret housed two big guns, mounted side by side. Ericsson had wanted 12-inch smoothbore Dahlgrens, but he settled for the only big guns available, 11-inch Dahlgrens.

The *Monitor* would be guided by her captain and helmsman from a small iron pilot house, which stood on the deck 55 feet forward of the turret. The pilot house had ⅝-inch-high eye slits on all sides. The *Monitor's* engine, another Ericsson invention, was connected to a crankshaft that drove a single

four-bladed propeller. The ship could make six knots. Her exhaust was vented through a smokestack that could be dismantled to prepare for battle.

On January 30, 1862, the *Monitor* made her maiden voyage in New York's East River. It was 18 days later than the contract had specified, but much sooner than anyone else had believed possible. With the aid of Northern industries, Ericsson had built his *Monitor* in half the time the Confederacy took to rebuild the *Merrimac*.

On February 25, the U.S. Navy commissioned the *Monitor* and appointed Lieutenant John Worden to command her. Worden, who had been captured by the Confederates early in the War and had recently been released in an exchange of prisoners, undertook to recruit 57 men for the *Monitor*. It was easy: When he appealed for volunteers aboard warships in New York Harbor, he got many more applicants than he needed.

On March 6, 1862, the *Monitor* left New York Harbor assisted by a tugboat and escorted by two gunboats. Worden's orders were to report to the squadron blockading Hampton Roads, then to proceed up the Potomac to protect Washington.

While the *Monitor* was heading south, the *Merrimac* departed Gosport accompanied by two small gunboats, the *Raleigh* and the *Beaufort*. The *Merrimac's* mission, known only to Franklin Buchanan and a few of his officers, was to attack the powerful Union

fleet at Hampton Roads: the 50-gun sailing frigate *St. Lawrence*, the 50-gun sailing frigate *Congress*, the 40-gun steam frigate *Minnesota*, the 40-gun steam frigate *Roanoke* and the 24-gun sailing sloop *Cumberland*.

Curious crowds lined the banks of the Elizabeth River to watch the *Merrimac* steam for the Roads. "Few, if any, entertained an exalted idea of our efficiency," noted ship's surgeon Dinwiddie Phillips, "and many predicted a total failure." One cynic shouted to the *Merrimac's* crew, "Go on with your old metallic coffin! She will never amount to anything else!"

The *Merrimac* was hard to steer and was even more sluggish than had been expected. "From the start we saw that she was slow, not over five knots," Lieutenant John Wood wrote. "She was as unmanageable as a waterlogged vessel." Buchanan ordered her to make way cautiously to keep from running aground in the shallow river.

At noon, after one hour of cautious steaming, the *Merrimac* passed Craney Island at the mouth of the Elizabeth River. Confederate troops along the shore burst into cheers at the sight of their strange craft. Buchanan outlined his plans to his officers. The *Merrimac* would first attack the *Cumberland* and the *Congress* off Newport News. Then she

Pierced by the *Merrimac's* ram and listing badly, the U.S.S. *Cumberland* fights on furiously under Lieutenant George Morris, who waves his sword and shouts orders through a speaking trumpet. In the brief exchange, 121 of the 376 men aboard the Federal warship were killed.

would swing eastward and go after the *Minnesota* and the *Roanoke*, several miles closer to Fort Monroe.

The *Merrimac* had been under way for about 90 minutes when the Federal gunboat *Zouave* sighted her. The *Zouave* opened fire. But the ironclad shrugged off the shells and closed to within a mile of the *Cumberland*, which was standing firm. Then the *Merrimac* fired her 7-inch bow gun. Her opening shell wounded several of the *Cumberland's* men. Her second exploded among a forward gun crew. It killed everyone except the powder boy and the gun captain, who lost both arms at the shoulder.

Shells from the *Cumberland*, the *Congress* and the Union Army batteries at Newport News glanced harmlessly off the *Merrimac's* sloping sides, which her crew had made slippery with buckets of hot pork fat. Those shells had no more effect, wrote a newspaper correspondent watching the attack from the shore, than "peas from a popgun."

Intending to dispatch the wounded *Cumberland* by ramming, Buchanan ordered full speed ahead. He used the entire mile separating the two ships to gain momentum. Three or four hundred yards from the *Cumberland*, the *Merrimac* came abreast of the *Congress* and the two ships exchanged broadsides.

The *Merrimac* kept coming straight toward the *Cumberland*. "As she came plowing through the water toward our port bow, she looked like a huge half-submerged crocodile," reported the *Cumberland's* pilot, A. B. Smith. "At her prow, I could see the iron ram. It was impossible for our vessel to get out of her way."

Inside the *Merrimac*, Chief Engineer H. A. Ramsey heard shells bouncing off the iron plating; apparently their fuses had been set for a longer range. He wrote: "They struck our sloping sides, were deflected upward to burst harmlessly in the air, or rolled down and fell hissing into the water, dashing spray up into our ports."[2]

The *Merrimac* broke through the protective barrier of timbers surrounding the *Cumberland's* anchorage and smashed into the Yankee's starboard side. The impact caused only a slight jarring inside the *Merrimac*, but it ripped open a gaping hole below the *Cumberland's* water line near the bow. The hole, Lieutenant Wood remembered, was "wide enough to drive in a horse and cart."

The doomed sloop listed sharply to starboard. Buchanan had ordered the engines reversed to pull the *Merrimac* free as soon as possible after ramming. But nothing happened. She was caught. Her engines labored and roared. The weight of the sinking *Cumberland* was taking the ironclad down too.

After a few tense seconds, the tidal current slued the *Merrimac* sideways and she pulled free. But her ram had broken off and remained embedded in the *Cumberland's* side —like the stinger of a wasp inside a victim, said Chief Engineer Ramsey.

Although the *Cumberland* was mortally wounded, she refused to give up the fight. Wrote the *Cumberland's* surgeon later: "The sanded deck is red and slippery with the blood of the wounded and the dying; they are dragged amidships. There is no one and no time to take them below. Delirium seizes the crew; they strip to their trousers; tie handkerchiefs around their heads, kick off their shoes; fight and yell like demons; load and fire at will."

Buchanan called on the *Cumberland* to surrender. Lieutenant George Morris, the *Cumberland's* commander, shouted back, "Never! I'll sink alongside." When the water had risen to the feet of the men on the gun deck, Morris yelled, "Save all who can!" Some men dived overboard and began swimming to shore. Others raced to the spar deck to continue fighting. All at once, the ship gave a lurch, and her bow went under. A heavy gun broke loose and pitched down the steeply slanting deck, crushing a sailor.

With a great roar, the *Cumberland* plunged down until her hull hit the sand 54 feet below. Her mainmast showed just above the waves, and atop it the ship's pennant still flew. "No ship was ever fought more gallantly," wrote Confederate Lieutenant Wood.

Buchanan determined to attack the *Congress*. He took the *Merrimac* a short way up the James River to have water deep enough to come about. The commander of the *Congress*, Lieutenant Joseph Smith Jr., son of the Commodore Smith on Welles's Ironclad Board, signaled to the *Zouave* to tow him into the shoals, where the deep-draft *Merrimac* could not follow and where Union artillery batteries would offer protection.

But by the time the *Zouave* had the *Congress* headed toward shore, the *Merrimac* was closing in astern. Joined by a group of Confederate gunboats, she poured round after round into the wooden vessel. Skipper Reaney of the *Zouave* reported that "blood was running from the *Congress* scuppers onto our deck like water on a wash-deck morning." Because of the angle at which she ran aground, the *Congress* could bring only two of her 50 guns to bear on the *Merrimac*. Both cannon were quickly knocked out of action.

Reduced to helplessness and with her young commander killed, the *Congress* ran up a white flag. Buchanan sent out two of his gunboats to receive the surrender. But the

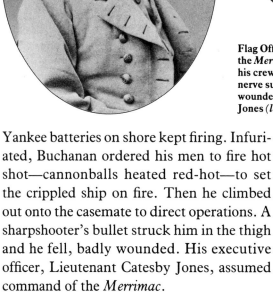

Flag Officer Franklin Buchanan (*above*), **captain of the** *Merrimac*, **was a man so stern that one of his crewmen remarked, "The sailor never lived with nerve sufficient to disobey him." After he was wounded, his command fell to Lieutenant Catesby Jones** (*left*), **who ably combated the** *Monitor*.

Yankee batteries on shore kept firing. Infuriated, Buchanan ordered his men to fire hot shot—cannonballs heated red-hot—to set the crippled ship on fire. Then he climbed out onto the casemate to direct operations. A sharpshooter's bullet struck him in the thigh and he fell, badly wounded. His executive officer, Lieutenant Catesby Jones, assumed command of the *Merrimac*.

With the *Cumberland* sunk and the *Congress* on fire, Jones determined to attack the *Minnesota*. That Federal frigate had run aground in the North Channel while her commander, Captain Van Brunt, was attempting to come to the aid of the *Cumberland* and the *Congress*. Frantically, Van Brunt signaled for the *Zouave* to tow him to safety. But as the *Zouave* steamed toward the frigate, a shot from the *Merrimac* carried away her rudder and one of her propeller blades, spinning her around. The gunboat, now facing the enemy, made an attempt to steam backward to the *Minnesota*.

"The scene was one of unsurpassed magnificence," wrote a Confederate Army offi-

Lieutenant John Worden *(above)* was appointed captain of the *Monitor* because of his reputation for aggressiveness and expert seamanship. After he was wounded dueling the *Merrimac*, he was replaced by Lieutenant S. Dana Greene *(right)*, who, said Worden, "fought the guns with great skill."

cer watching from a nearby island. "The bright afternoon sun shone upon the glancing waters. The fortifications of Newport News were seen swarming with soldiers, now idle spectators of a conflict far beyond the range of their batteries, and the flames were just bursting from the abandoned *Congress*. The stranded *Minnesota* seemed a huge monster at bay."

But it was now ebb tide and nightfall was approaching. If the *Merrimac* were to try to get close enough to dispatch the *Minnesota*, she might run aground herself. The pilots on the *Merrimac* refused to take the risk, so Jones broke off the attack and headed toward home. They would return in the morning to finish the job.

In the last minutes of daylight, the *Merrimac* dropped anchor off Sewell's Point. Despite the wounding of Buchanan, the Confederates were jubilant. They had won a smashing victory. In four and a half hours, they had destroyed two large Federal warships. Numerous hits from 100 heavy Federal cannon afloat and ashore had disabled two

of the *Merrimac's* guns, riddled her smokestack and swept away almost everything on the outside. But the *Merrimac* had lost only two men killed and 19 wounded, and her armor was hardly damaged. "After making preparations for the next day's fight," wrote Lieutenant Wood, "we slept at our guns, dreaming of other victories in the morning."

As the *Merrimac's* crew settled down for the night, the telegraph flashed the news of the Union disaster across the North. Early the next morning, President Lincoln called an emergency meeting of his Cabinet. "The *Merrimac* will change the whole character of the War," declared Secretary of War Edwin Stanton, a fierce critic of Navy Secretary Welles. "She will destroy, seriatim, every naval vessel; she will lay all the cities on the seaboard under contribution."

In reply, Welles confidently read a telegram from Lieutenant John Worden, announcing that the *Monitor* had arrived in Hampton Roads after sunset on March 8. But the message did not reassure Lincoln's Cabinet. Stanton felt that "Ericsson's folly," armed with only two guns, had little chance against the *Merrimac*. Gazing out the window at the Potomac, he declared, "Not unlikely, we shall have a shell or cannonball from one of her guns in the White House before we leave this room." Afterward, he fired off telegrams to the governors of seacoast states: "MAN YOUR GUNS. BLOCK YOUR HARBORS. THE *MERRIMAC* IS COMING."

Welles remained confident. But if he had been aware of the *Monitor's* harrowing trip south, he would have worried more. Twice, the *Monitor* had come close to sinking in rough weather. In fact, she was not nearly as seaworthy as Ericsson believed.

After he entered the Roads, Lieutenant Worden had boarded the command ship *Roanoke* at 9 p.m. and reported to Captain John Marston, the acting commander of the North Atlantic Blockading Squadron. On orders from Marston, Worden and the *Monitor* set out to protect the *Minnesota;* they proceeded to the grounded frigate off Newport News, guided by light from the burning *Congress*. At midnight, the *Monitor* pulled alongside her charge and dropped anchor.

Worden and his men were exhausted. No one had eaten anything but hardtack or slept a wink in two days. They needed sleep to be ready for a life-or-death struggle on the morrow. But they got little sleep. Sometime after 1 a.m., the *Congress* blew up in a series of spectacular explosions. "Her powder tanks seemed to explode," Lieutenant S. Dana Greene, Executive Officer of the *Monitor*, recalled, "each shower of sparks rivaling the other in its height, until they appeared to reach the zenith—a grand but mournful sight." No one was able to sleep for the rest of the night; the men stayed tensely alert, ready for any emergency.

At dawn, just as a light fog was lifting, Lieutenant Catesby Jones took the *Merrimac* out of anchorage off Sewell's Point. He moved the ironclad slowly into the channel and headed westward across the Roads toward the intended victim.

Exuberant Confederate spectators lined the banks. Some brave ones piled into small boats and hurried toward the action; they wanted to witness at close hand the destruction of the whole hated Yankee blockade.

As the *Merrimac* neared her objective, a bizarre little ship darted out from behind the huge *Minnesota*. A Confederate observer, approaching in a rowboat, later wrote: "No

The *Monitor* and the *Merrimac* exchange shots at close range during their duel at Hampton Roads on March 9, 1862. The frigate *Minnesota*, which the *Monitor* was ordered to protect, sits grounded at right. In the distance lie the wrecks of the *Congress* and the *Cumberland*, which had succumbed to the *Merrimac* the day before.

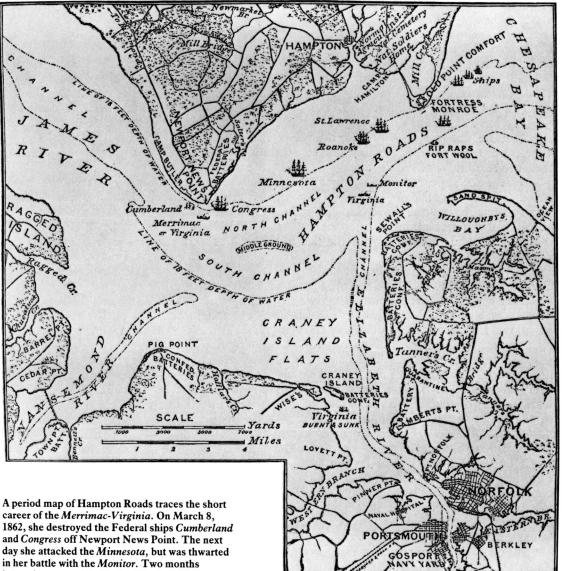

A period map of Hampton Roads traces the short career of the *Merrimac-Virginia*. On March 8, 1862, she destroyed the Federal ships *Cumberland* and *Congress* off Newport News Point. The next day she attacked the *Minnesota*, but was thwarted in her battle with the *Monitor*. Two months later, she was scuttled in the Elizabeth River.

Playing cards manufactured New York to cash in on the *Merrima Monitor* duel display the tw ironclads, a drummer boy and Zouave in place of the convention suits and numerical pip

words can express the surprise with which we beheld this strange craft, whose appearance was tersely and graphically described by the exclamation of one of my oarsmen, 'A tin can on a shingle!' "

The officers on the *Merrimac* knew at once that the strange craft was Ericsson's *Monitor*, which they had long been expecting at Hampton Roads. "She could not possibly have made her appearance at a more inopportune time for us," said Lieutenant Wood in rueful hindsight. But at the time, the *Monitor* was hardly intimidating. "She appeared but a pigmy compared with the lofty frigate which she guarded."

Aboard the *Monitor,* in the eerie glow of lanterns, each man waited at his post, "fixed like a statue," according to Paymaster Wil-

liam Keeler. "The most profound silence reigned. If there had been a coward's heart there its throb would have been audible, so intense was the stillness. We were enclosed in what we supposed to be an impenetrable armor. We knew that a powerful foe was about to meet us. Ours was an untried experiment and our enemy's first fire might make it a coffin for us all."

The *Merrimac* opened fire at precisely 8:06 a.m. Her first shot passed directly over the *Monitor* and smashed into the side of the *Minnesota*, which answered with a full broadside of heavy guns. To the men inside the *Monitor*, the firing guns and exploding shells were deafening. "The noise," said Keeler, "would not quiet the nerves of an excitable person."

When the *Merrimac* reached close range, she turned sideways and delivered a broadside. Heavy shells struck the *Monitor's* turret and exploded harmlessly against the thick iron plating. "A look of confidence passed over the men's faces," Lieutenant Greene remembered. "We believed the *Merrimac* would not repeat the work she had accomplished the day before."

For the next four hours—"which seemed three times as long," an observer said later—the ironclads exchanged blows at ranges varying from a few yards to half a mile. Like boxers, they circled and probed for weak spots, moving in and out. But at whatever range, neither could hurt the other.

Each ironclad had certain advantages and disadvantages. Because of her shallow draft, better engines and smaller size, the *Monitor* was a faster, more maneuverable and more elusive target. But the *Merrimac* had greater firepower. Her 10 guns could be fired and reloaded every five minutes. It took up to

eight minutes to fire, reload and run out the *Monitor's* two guns.

The *Monitor* had other problems. Her voice tube, through which Worden in the pilot house gave directions to Lieutenant Greene at the guns in the turret, stopped working. Two crew members passed the word between them. Even when Worden managed to inform Greene of the *Merrimac's* bearing, Greene had no quick or accurate way to bring his guns to bear on the target. The men had made white marks on the port and starboard sides of the deck so that when their gun turret turned, they could tell which side their guns were facing. But in the grime and smoke of battle, the marks soon disappeared and the gunners became disoriented. This presented Greene with a terrible problem. His only view of the world outside was over the muzzles of the guns; most of his shots had to be fired in a hurry, when the target was briefly visible. Greene also had to be careful not to fire close to the *Monitor's* bow for fear that a shell might accidentally hit the pilot house.

At one point, the *Merrimac's* deep draft almost brought her to disaster. She hit bottom and became stuck in the sand. The *Monitor* closed in at an angle that avoided the Confederate's guns and pumped shot after shot into the casemate. The *Merrimac's* engineers tied down the safety valves on the engines and threw every combustible they could find into the boiler fires in an effort to gain extra power. At last, after 15 hair-raising minutes, the *Merrimac* thrashed free and the sparring resumed.

Soon afterward, as Lieutenant Jones came down from the spar deck, he noticed that some of the gun crews were not firing and demanded an explanation.

The *Merrimac*, trapped between the blockade and advancing Union soldiers, blows up after being set afire by her crew off Craney Island, Virginia, on May 11, 1862. Her captain, criticized for destroying the famous vessel, asked for a court-martial to prove that he had no other choice. He was tried and exonerated.

"Our powder is very precious," replied the lieutenant in charge. The two hours he had spent firing at the *Monitor* without noticeable effect led him to add, "I can do her about as much damage by snapping my thumb at her every two minutes and a half."

Jones thereupon decided that he would have to ram the *Monitor*, even though his iron prow was broken. It took him an hour to maneuver into position; when he finally attacked, the nimble *Monitor* swerved, taking only a harmless glancing blow. Then, at point-blank range, Greene fired two shots that struck halfway up the *Merrimac's* casemate. The crews of the after guns were bowled over by the concussive force, and men bled from the ears and nose.

Shortly after noon, the *Merrimac* fired the most damaging shot of the battle at a range of no more than 10 yards. The shell exploded on the forward side of the *Monitor's* pilot house. Lieutenant Worden was pressing his face against the eye slits when the shell struck. He staggered backward, temporarily blinded in his right eye and permanently in his left, with half of his face forever blackened. Though the only damage to the ship was a slight buckling of the pilot-house roof, Worden thought that the damage was far greater and ordered his helmsman to sheer off. Lieutenant Greene and other officers led Worden to his wardroom.

"I leave it with you, do what you think best," Worden told his crew. "I cannot

Lighted by a distress rocket, crewmen of the foundering *Monitor* abandon ship in a lifeboat from the steamer *Rhode Island* during a nighttime storm off Cape Hatteras on December 30, 1862. Most of the *Monitor's* sailors were picked up, but 16 men went down with the ironclad.

see, but do not mind me. Save the *Minnesota* if you can."

The officers consulted and decided to continue the fight. Greene, returning to the pilot house, discovered that the ship had run into water much too shallow for the *Merrimac* to follow. He headed the *Monitor* back toward her enemy.

Aboard the *Merrimac*, Lieutenant Jones watched the *Monitor's* retreat in utter frustration. His foe's departure gave him a chance to finish off the *Minnesota*. But the tide was going out, and his pilots told him he could not close on the frigate without running aground. Besides, the *Merrimac* was leaking and her ammunition was nearly exhausted.

Consoling himself with the thought that the *Merrimac* had driven the *Monitor* from the field, Jones set his course for home. On board the *Monitor*, Greene saw the Confederate ironclad steaming toward Sewell's Point and, firing off several shots, was satisfied to let the fight end. It was no part of his duty to give chase; the *Monitor's* strict orders had been to provide protection for the *Minnesota*, and this she had done.

Soon both crews, realizing they were out of range of each other's guns, raced to their hatches to breathe fresh air. The men of the *Monitor* were well past fatigue. Lieutenant Greene declared: "I had been up so long, and been under such a state of excitement, that my nervous system was completely run down . . . my nerves and muscles twitched as though electric shocks were continually passing through them. I lay down and tried to sleep. I might as well have tried to fly."

Tactically, the duel between the ironclads had ended in a draw. But even the Confederates agreed that the *Monitor*, by preventing the destruction of the Union's wooden ships, had won a strategic victory. Almost everything else about the battle was disputed.

Second guessing began almost at once. What if the *Merrimac* had concentrated her fire on the *Monitor's* pilot house from the beginning? What if her prow had been intact when she rammed the *Monitor?* Word leaked out that the Navy Department had cautiously ordered the *Monitor* to reduce her powder charges from the specified 30 pounds to only 15 pounds out of fear that her big guns would burst. Ericsson was outraged by the order. He asserted bitterly: "If they had kept off at a distance of 200 yards and held her gun exactly level, the 30-pound charges would have gone clear through." Later experiments proved him correct.

For the next two months, the *Monitor* protected the Federal fleet at Hampton Roads. The *Merrimac* underwent extensive repairs at the Gosport Navy Yard, then came out to fight again on April 11; she intended to cover some wooden gunboats in their planned attempt to take the *Monitor* by boarding. But the *Monitor* and other vessels of the fleet remained below Fort Monroe. After exchanging a few shots with shore batteries, the Confederates canceled the attack.

Neither of the two ironclads survived the year. On May 10 the Confederates vacated Norfolk, and the Gosport Navy Yard fell back into Union hands. The *Merrimac* was scuttled to prevent her capture, and on the 30th of December the *Monitor* sank in a gale off Cape Hatteras, losing many members of the current crew.

Nevertheless, it was now clear that the age of the ironclad had arrived. Thanks to the success of the *Merrimac*, Mallory was able to pry two million dollars from the straitened Confederate Congress to buy ironclads abroad and build them at home. By February of 1863, the Confederates had finished eight ironclads and had begun several more. In the vastly richer North, Welles received $13 million for ironclads alone, and the Navy ordered 56 monitors.

So the ironclad proved not to be the ultimate weapon that Northerners had feared it was and that Southerners had hoped it was. It was just another new weapon that could be marvelously effective but adequately countered by others of its kind; indeed, an ironclad was probably more dangerous to its own crew than to an enemy ironclad. Nor did the ironclads change the general character of the Civil War at sea, which would be fought to the end chiefly by wooden ships.

The most dramatic effect of the clash at Hampton Roads was the public excitement it generated north and south. People everywhere were fascinated by the unattractive new vessels and lionized the men who served on them, especially those who had fought aboard the *Merrimac* and the *Monitor*. All that praise for fighting the battle seemed misplaced to Lieutenant William Keeler. "Anyone can fight behind impenetrable armor," he wrote. "The credit, if any is due, is in daring to undertake the trip."

The Strange New "Fighting Machines"

Shortly after the *Monitor's* success against the *Merrimac* in March 1862, the British magazine *Punch* waggishly declared that the old seaman's expression "Shiver my timbers!" would have to be changed to "Unrivet my bolts!" The little joke seemed apropos, for the United States Navy began building dozens of the strange ironclads in 13 classes based on inventor John Ericsson's original monitor design.

With their shallow-draft hulls designed exclusively as a platform for rotating gun turrets, the monitors broke with 500 years of naval architecture; Ericsson aptly described them not as ships but as "fighting machines." From keel up, they were intended to serve one purpose only—to bring their guns into battle, primarily in shallow rivers and sheltered harbors—and were virtually useless for anything else. Everything about the ironclads embodied the latest technology.

The men who fought aboard the monitors were different, too, from the old seamen skilled at furling sails and splicing rope. For crew, the Navy chose landlubberly craftsmen: machinists, blacksmiths and boilermakers. For officers, engineering became a requisite to advancement.

Old Navy men bitterly criticized the monitors' poor ventilation and their unseaworthiness. But Northerners were excited by the grim, greasy little ironclads and the nautical revolution they represented. "About a week ago," young Henry Adams proudly wrote of the *Monitor-Merrimac* battle, "the British discovered that their whole wooden navy was useless."

Workmen in San Francisco Bay assemble a monitor, later named the *Camanche,* to patrol the West coast. The parts for the ironclad had been manufactured in New Jersey and shipped in sections to spare the unseaworthy ship the long and dangerous journey around Cape Horn.

New York dignitaries stand on the deck of the *Modoc* at its launching ceremony in 1865. Designed with so little freeboard that its deck was nearly awash in calm seas, this class of monitor was a failure. Only eight of the 20 contracted for were commissioned, and five of them were converted into torpedo boats by removing their ponderous turrets to make them more buoyant.

Officials await the launching of the *Dictator*, prototype of the War's largest class of monitors, at the Delameter Iron Works in New York on the 26th of December, 1863. The *Dictator*'s 312-foot hull was protected by six inches of armor.

The *Onondaga*, one of five double-turret monitors built during the War, lies at anchor in Virginia's James River in 1864. The ship was 226 feet long and wa

armed with two 15-inch and two 8-inch cannon. The tarpaulins over the deck were rigged by the men to provide some shade from the blistering Southern sun.

The engine room of the *Camanche* was crammed with machinery and piping to regulate steam and pressure. To provide ventilation, engine rooms in the monitors operated at two pounds above normal atmospheric pressure and had one of the world's first forced-draft systems.

The anchor well on the *Catskill* was cut out of the ironclad's overhanging bow. As specified by designer Ericsson, the anchor could be raised or lowered by windlass from inside the ship so that the crewmen would not be exposed to enemy fire.

Men of the engineering gang aboard the *Lehigh*, one of 10 improved monitors designed by Ericsson in 1862, forge a replacement part on the deck of the ironclad. Their portable forge and anvil, standard equipment on monitors, were also used to repair damaged sheet armor.

Appraising the battle damage, officers of the *Monitor* examine dents in the turret made by the *Merrimac's* shot and shells. Partially visible in the background is a new, slope-sided pilot house, built after the original square one was wrecked in the fight.

A gun crew on the *Lehigh* drills with a 12-pounder howitzer that was used to repel boarders during close fights with Confederate troops. The gun was designed for quick assembly; its parts could be easily stored below.

A Fearful Warship Made of Junk

"You must not expect too much of the *Albemarle*," wrote a crew member in 1864, "for she is the poorest ironclad in the Confederacy." The *Albemarle*'s origins were humble indeed. The 158-foot ram was built in a cornfield, and her armor was made from scrap iron salvaged by her captain, Commander James W. Cooke. Yet this make-shift warship threatened Union control of the Carolina coast, sinking, disabling or scaring off Federal gunboats even when outnumbered seven to one.

The *Albemarle*'s startling successes began on her maiden voyage, when she clashed with two Federal gunboats, the *Miami* and the *Southfield*. Cooke sent his ship steaming

Crewmen abandon the sinking U.S.S. *Southfield (foreground)* as her companion gunboat, the *Miami (right)*, unleashes a futile fusillade against the armored *Albemarle*

full tilt toward the Yankees. The ram caromed off the *Miami* and ran her iron prow 10 feet into the side of the *Southfield*, quickly sinking the gunboat. The *Miami*'s captain, Charles Flusser, was flukishly killed by his ship's own ricocheting shell. The ship then fled and her crew spread the news of the fearsome new Confederate weapon.

Confederate Commander James W. Cooke (*above*) of the *Albemarle* and Lieutenant Commander Charles W. Flusser of the U.S.S. *Miami* met in battle on April 19, 1864.

New Victories for the "Albemarle"

The *Albemarle's* triumphant debut alarmed Rear Admiral Samuel P. Lee, commander of the U.S. North Atlantic Blockading Squadron. To stop the Confederate ironclad, Lee dispatched seven gunboats under Captain Melancton Smith. When the *Albemarle* emerged from the Roanoke River on May 5, 1864, Smith was waiting there with his little fleet.

As the repaired *Miami* and supporting ships distracted the Confederates, the sidewheeler *Sassacus* raced in at full speed and rammed into the *Albemarle's* starboard side. With the vessels interlocked, their crews traded cannon shots point-blank.

While 100-pound solid shot bounced ineffectually off the ram's four-inch-thick iron hide, a round from the *Albemarle* pierced the *Sassacus'* boiler, engulfing the Union crew in clouds of scalding steam. In the ensuing pandemonium, the ships drifted apart and Cooke fought his way back to the safety of the Roanoke River. The *Albemarle* had only minor damage and three wounded. The Federals had four men dead and 25 wounded. The *Sassacus* was crippled and several other ships were damaged.

Admiral Lee, seeing that the ironclad could not be beaten by the usual tactics, summoned Lieutenant William B. Cushing, a 21-year-old daredevil famous for raids behind enemy lines. By chance, Cushing had a personal motive—to avenge the death of Charles Flusser, who had been his teacher, commanding officer and friend.

The *Sassacus*, her bow embedded in the side of the *Albemarle*, batters at the Confederate ironclad with rounds from her 100-pounder Parrott rifles and 9-inch Dahlgren guns. The *Albemarle* withstood 54 direct hits, and the captain of the *Sassacus* pronounced her "more formidable than the *Atlanta* or the *Merrimac.*"

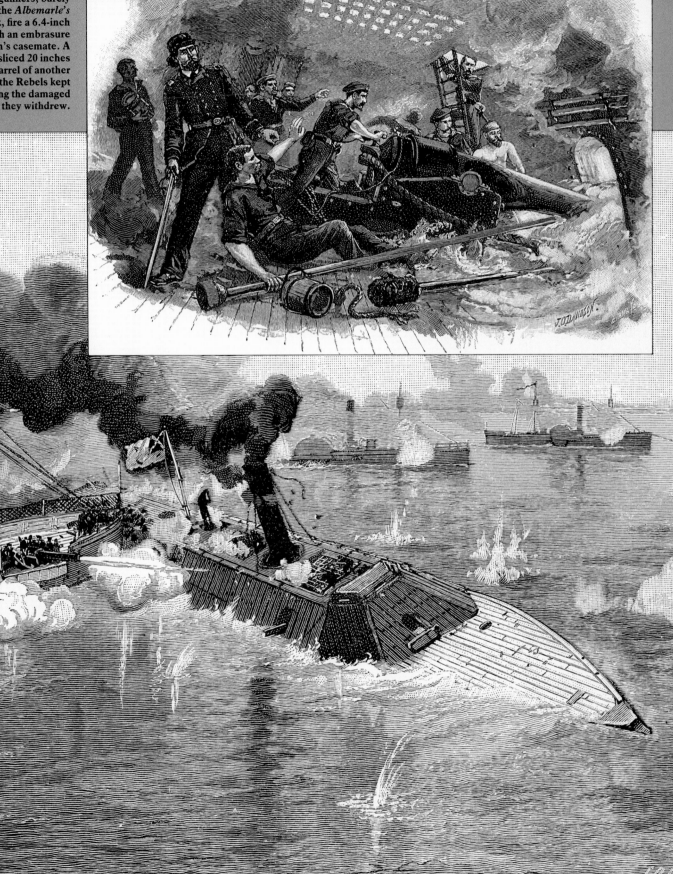

Confederate gunners, barely balancing on the *Albemarle's* pitching deck, fire a 6.4-inch gun through an embrasure in the ram's casemate. A Union shell sliced 20 inches from the barrel of another cannon, but the Rebels kept right on firing the damaged gun as they withdrew.

The weapon Cushing used against the *Albemarle* was a buoyant torpedo at the end of a wooden spar. The spar was lowered by a pulley. A tug on one lanyard released the torpedo, which was exploded under the *Albemarle* by a tug on a second lanyard.

Staring into an *Albemarle* cannon, Lieutenant Cushing triggers the torpedo extended from the bow of his boat. The blast tore a six-foot hole in the ironclad.

Lieutenant Cushing's Explosive Revenge

Near midnight on October 27, 1864, Lieutenant Cushing and a hand-picked crew of 14 Union volunteers entered the Roanoke River in a 30-foot boat that had a long torpedo-launching apparatus *(inset, left)* set into the bow. The little band of Federals headed for the heavily guarded *Albemarle*, eight miles upriver.

It was 3 a.m. when Cushing spotted the dim outline of the *Albemarle*. Before long his boat was challenged from the ironclad. His men answered facetiously, and Confederate sentries opened fire with small arms. Undeterred, Cushing raced in and sent his boat crashing over a log barrier protecting the ironclad. He lowered the long spar, thrusting the torpedo into the water under the *Albemarle*.

Cushing stood up. Bullets nicked his hand and tore his uniform coat, but he tugged on the triggering lanyard. His torpedo exploded, mortally wounding the ironclad. A moment later the *Albemarle's* cannon smashed the boat, flinging the raiders into the river. Most were captured. Cushing was one of two Federals to get away.

LIEUTENANT WILLIAM B. CUSHING

Pro-Union sightseers celebrate atop the casemate of the *Albemarle*, sunk in a shallow stretch of the Roanoke River outside Plymouth, North Carolina. For sinking the ironclad, Lieutenant Cushing received a vote of thanks from the United States Congress, $56,000 in prize money and a promotion to lieutenant commander.

A Game of Hare and Hounds

The steamer *Cecile*, a lean, low ship painted the color of fog and laden with 700 bales of cotton, departed the North Carolina port of Wilmington on January 11, 1862, pushed down the Cape Fear River and anchored at twilight near its mouth. The *Cecile's* master, Lieutenant John Newland Maffitt of the Confederate States Navy, peered through his telescope at the river entrance, where enemy ships lay in wait, dark and menacing shapes on the horizon. That night Maffitt would brave the Federal cordon on his first voyage as a blockade-runner.

When the moon disappeared from the night sky, Maffitt weighed anchor slowly and carefully so that the chains did not rattle. The *Cecile*, her lights blacked out and her sidewheels barely turning, inched down the narrow inlet toward the Atlantic. Ahead, anchored in the channel, two Federal warships barred her way to freedom. "Instantly out of the gloom emerges the somber phantom form of the blockading fleet," Maffitt wrote later. "The moment of trial is at hand; firmness and decision are essential for the emergency. Dashing between the two at anchor, we pass so near as to excite astonishment at our nondiscovery."

Just as the *Cecile's* crew began to breathe more easily, flares sent up by the Federal vessels lit the sky and exposed the Confederate runner. Under the guns of the enemy, Lieutenant Maffitt chose immediately between surrender and flight, shouting to his engineer for full speed. As shot whistled through the ship's rigging and shells exploded around her, the *Cecile* churned the black water to foam with her paddles. Suddenly the vessel shuddered from a hit: Two of the crew were wounded and several bales of deckside cotton were knocked overboard. But Maffitt pressed on, and soon his ship steamed out of range of the guns, into the engulfing darkness.

Three days later, Maffitt arrived at his destination, Nassau in the Bahamas, and exchanged his cargo of cotton for 900 barrels of gunpowder. Then he charted a return course for Wilmington. Running the blockade the opposite way, the *Cecile* once again came under heavy fire from Federal gunboats, and once again she escaped them. Had a shell penetrated her hull this time, the gunpowder in the hold would have blown the *Cecile* to splinters. As it was, the explosives were later used by the Confederate forces at the Battle of Shiloh.

Maffitt's first triumph was no fluke. For the next five months he retraced the perilous route numerous times, taking out cotton and bringing back arms, ammunition, medicine and clothing for the Confederacy. Luck was on his side, but good fortune alone could not have protected the *Cecile* from disaster so often.

Maffitt, in fact, was an expert seaman with all the experience he needed for this job. Before joining the Confederate Navy in 1861, the North Carolinian had served for 29 years in the United States Navy, 14 of them

The Great Seal of the Confederacy, engraved in silver in Great Britain, was smuggled through the blockade in 1864. The seal bears the martial figure of George Washington encircled by cotton, tobacco, rice and sugar cane—crops exported by blockade-runners, who returned to the South with guns and ammunition. The Latin motto reads: "With God as defender."

on duty surveying and mapping the Atlantic coast. He was perhaps the world's leading authority on the shifting sand bars, currents and tides of the Carolinas—an inestimable boon to a blockade-runner. He had more than his fair share of grit, daring and a gambler's instinct for good odds.

All the assets Maffitt brought to the task had become, by the second year of the War, prerequisites for survival in blockade-running. The Federals had made the business a perilous game. Their Navy, in 1862, steadily tightened its grip on the coastline of the Confederacy. In April, U.S. warships in the Gulf of Mexico captured the South's premier port, New Orleans. Although Mobile, Alabama, and Galveston, Texas, were still open to blockade-runners, neither was an attractive port of call: Mobile Bay's narrow entrance was easy to guard and therefore dangerous, and Galveston was too remote from the heartland of the Confederacy. The coasts of Florida were also unsatisfactory because they lacked road and rail links to the heart of the South. On the Atlantic side, Fort Pulaski, the strong point that controlled access to the port of Savannah upriver, yielded to the Federal Army in the spring. New Bern, North Carolina, also fell to Union forces that season, as did Fort Macon, which commanded the approaches to Beaufort, North Carolina. Before the summer was over, the Confederacy was reduced to primary dependence on only two portals to the trading world: Charleston, South Carolina, and Wilmington, North Carolina.

Even as Southern ports were captured or cut off, more Federal vessels became available for patrolling. Additional ships, fresh from Northern shipyards, joined the picketing squadrons every month; in 1862 the United States Navy grew from 264 to 427 ships, then to 588 in 1863. Also in 1862, the Navy began to assign new monitors to the blockading squadrons to protect the wooden ships from Confederate ironclads. And the newly established coaling and supply stations at Cape Hatteras and Port Royal ensured that the blockading ships remained longer at their stations.

The growing might of the U.S. Navy pushed amateur blockade-runners out of business. Their small, slow craft—worn-out steamers and pilot boats—were easily run down and seized, and others were discouraged from taking the chance. The sea lanes were left to the professional blockade-runners, both military and civilian. Some Confederate Navy officers, such as Maffitt, commanded ships that were owned or leased by their government. They were patriots who braved every terror the sea could toss up to bring the Confederacy the necessities for waging its struggle.

Far more numerous were the civilian captains who sailed their own vessels or those owned by one of the investment syndicates, most of them British, that sprang up to tap a deep well of potential profit. Although they were generally sympathetic to the cause of the South, the investors and their hired captains were primarily concerned with making money. Their preferred cargoes were not guns and powder, but luxuries—French Cognac, Madeira wine, Belgian silk, perfumes and cigars—that brought the highest profits at auctions held in Southern ports. And profit they did: as much as $425,000 for a single round trip between Wilmington and Nassau.

On such wealth were built whole fleets to defy the blockade. Millionaires were made in a month. And as the business evolved, the blockade-runners grew more sophisticated in their contest with the U.S. Navy, developing new techniques and vessels designed especially for the job.

Ships that had been built or converted for blockade-running sacrificed seaworthiness in favor of speed and maneuverability. Shallow draft enabled such vessels to dart into coves or inlets where the deeper-draft Federal ships could not follow. The lines of these runners were uncommonly sharp and narrow—length was as much as nine times the beam—so that the hull could knife through the water.

Profiles were kept low to make the vessels inconspicuous. A runner's hull rose only a few feet out of the water and her superstructure was kept rudimentary. On deck, funnels could be telescoped down to hide them, and the hulls were painted a dull gray to blend with the sea. Crew and passenger quarters were spartan: Cargo space was the first consideration.

Though most of these vessels could make headway under canvas and had stubby masts for a sail or two, their primary motive force was steam. Engines were big and powerful, some having enough brawn to push the craft to a top speed of 18 knots—much faster than nearly all the U.S. Navy's craft. The grade of coal used for fuel was crucial. Clean-burning anthracite coal was the favorite because it produced no telltale smoke. But since most of the anthracite coal came from Northern mines, it remained in short supply, and Welsh hard coal was most often carried. The soft, bituminous coal from the mines of the South was employed only as a last resort: It sent up clouds of dense black smoke.

Such tactical refinements became increasingly important for the runners as their enemy grew stronger and their ports were eliminated one by one. On September 7, 1863, Morris Island, whose batteries commanded the southern entrance to Charleston Harbor, fell to Union forces and that port became a bad risk for runners. Wilmington, 17 miles up the Cape Fear River (*map, pages 2-3*), became the first choice.

The geography of the Wilmington area favored the blockade-runners. Smith Island divided the Cape Fear River at its mouth into two channels: New Inlet on the north, protected by the guns of Fort Fisher, and the main channel to the south, guarded by Fort Caswell. After leaving Wilmington, a runner could sail down the Cape Fear River to the little town of Smithville, near the mouth of the river, and reconnoiter the Federal positions before choosing between the two routes. On the seaward side of Smith Island, the treacherous Frying Pan Shoals extended 10 miles into the Atlantic, requiring a 40-mile trip by sea from one entrance to the other. This meant that the U.S. Navy had to maintain two separate blockading squadrons to guard each channel of the river; a minimum of 50 ships were needed to cover Wilmington.

Outward bound from Wilmington, the blockade-runners usually charted course for one of several islands that served as neutral points for the transshipment of goods abroad. Most took their cargoes to the British ports of St. George on Bermuda or Nassau in the Bahamas, both of which were about three days distant. Similarly, runners from Gulf ports headed for Havana.

These island way stations served several purposes. They permitted the shippers to employ two specialized kinds of vessels, each perfectly suited to its own task: the deep-draft, ocean-worthy freighters for the long voyage to and from Europe, and the shallow-draft speedsters for the precarious runs through the U.S. Navy cordons around the Southern ports. The neutrality of the islands was also convenient: If a runner was stopped on the high seas by the Federals, she was less likely to be confiscated if her papers showed that her destination was a neutral port of call.

To elude the Federal blockaders close to the coast, the runners used a set of tactics ingeniously devised to meet changing circumstances. To begin with, the runners timed their departures from Nassau or Bermuda in order to have a moonless night and a high tide for their final dash through the cordon and into port. Then lights became critical in the game of hare and hounds. In the early days of the blockade, the runners were able to use the well-lighted ships of the Federal squadron as guide markers. When the Federal commanders realized their mistake, they blacked out their ships except for a single lantern left aglow on the senior officer's vessel, which remained anchored in the center of the fleet as a marker.

Before long, the blockade-runners learned of this arrangement in Southern ports or from the sympathizers and informers who

Shallow-draft blockade-runners ride at anchor in the bustling harbor of St. George, Bermuda, waiting to take on cargoes from lumbering, deep-draft transatlantic ships. In a single month in 1863, runners from Bermuda delivered to Southern ports 110,000 British and Austrian rifles, 21,000 British muskets and 129 cannon.

thrived on the docks of Nassau and Bermuda. Thereupon that single light became invaluable as a beacon on which the runners could get their bearings. When the Federals, in turn, discovered that they were only aiding the enemy, they changed the position of the lighted vessel, luring many a runner onto the shoals.

The hare-and-hounds game had other permutations and subtleties. At one point the blockading ships were ordered, upon spotting a runner, to send up a flare in the direction of the quarry's course in order to guide the pursuit. It did not take the runners long to counter this plan. They bought and took aboard rockets of the same type. In the midst of Federal ships, a runner would simply fire a flare at right angles to his course, sending his pursuers on a fruitless chase.

For all their firepower and superiority in numbers, the blockading ships had very few advantages. The runners always possessed the element of surprise, and the Federal ships were handicapped by their reactive role. Many a runner slipped through undetected by hugging the shore, where the ship was practically invisible and the noise of her engine was drowned by the breaking waves. When a runner was spotted, a Federal warship found it nearly impossible, in the pitch-black night on a heaving sea, to start her engine or put up sail quickly enough to head off a vessel that was speeding through the darkness at 18 knots. Indeed the Federals were hard put merely to bring their guns to bear accurately on their swift quarry. And the runners almost never surrendered unless hit by the Federals' fire.

The monotony and discomfort of life on board the blockading ships added to the frus-

On blockade duty in Southern waters, the famous racing yacht *America* (*left*) fires a rocket in the direction taken by a fleeing blockade-runner. Guided by such signals, U.S. warships patrolling farther out at sea set their courses to head off the runner. Below, a Federal gunboat closes in for the kill as a blockade-runner tries to escape.

trations of the officers and men of the U.S. Navy. Blockade duty, Rear Admiral Samuel F. Du Pont admitted, was "the most onerous service in the world." Many sailors spent months within sight of land without ever setting foot ashore. They polished brass, drilled at their guns and stood watch, enduring sweltering summers and gale-ridden, freezing winters off the Atlantic coast. Standing orders specified that the men stay at their battle stations when their vessel was chasing a suspected runner—whether the chase lasted two hours or two days.

The difficult duty returned few rewards. Pay was miserable—a crewman on blockade station earned just $16 per month. Only if a sailor was lucky enough to participate in the capture of a runner could he truly profit by his labors.

The awarding of prize money followed an official hearing to determine whether a seized ship was indeed a blockade-runner. Once a ship had been captured and taken into port, a special prize court examined its papers, inspected its cargo and interviewed witnesses before making a ruling. If the seizure was deemed legal—usually the case— the ship was sold, often to the U.S. government for blockade duty, and the cargo was auctioned off. The government kept half the prize money; the commander of the regional blockading squadron got 5 per cent of each prize and the local squadron commodore got 1 per cent. The rest was divided into 20 equal shares: The captain of the capturing ship received three shares; officers and midshipmen divided 10; and the enlisted men split the remaining seven among themselves.

Some men got rich for half a day's work. For the bloodless and uneventful capture of the blockade-runner *Hope*, the captain of

the tugboat *Eolus* received $13,164, and the crew members got more than $1,000 each. A few days later the same crewmen earned $2,000 apiece when their ship assisted in the taking of the *Lady Sterling*, a runner that turned out to be worth half a million dollars in prize court.

High-ranking Navy officers made a fortune in prize money. Rear Admiral Samuel P. Lee, for more than two years the commander of the North Atlantic Blockading Squadron, banked almost $110,000. In his months on patrol, Admiral David Dixon Porter amassed $91,528. In all, the United States government distributed well over $10 million in prize money. This bonanza prompted one Northern magazine to remark that the blockaders were animated by "Pride, Patriotism and Pocket."

The blockade-runners took their chances not just for money or patriotism but also for adventure and fame. For Southerners and their sympathizers, the trade assumed the proportions of an epic whose protagonists, the ship captains, possessed superhuman qualities: "The cunning of a fox, the patience of a Job, and the bravery of a Spartan warrior," as a Confederate veteran put it.

Such was heady stuff, and it quickened the pulse of many a young man with a taste for derring-do and dreams of gold. One of them was a young Englishman named Thomas Taylor who in 1862 was buried in boredom as an assistant for a firm of Liverpudlian merchants. "I had nothing to hope for," Taylor wrote in his memoirs, "beyond a dim chance of a partnership abroad in the future." So when the firm bought shares in a blockade-runner and asked Taylor if he would like to accompany the ship as supercargo (owner's representative), he fairly leaped at the chance.

Taylor's first voyage west was a dismal trip in a worn-out former cattle boat so unsuitable for blockade-running that it was leased as a towboat at Nassau. But when Taylor returned to Liverpool, a far superior ship, then under construction, awaited him.

Completed in the beginning of 1863, the *Banshee* was one of the first steel ships ever to be constructed for Atlantic trade. She was 214 feet long and 20 feet wide, and she drew only eight feet of water. Her captain, Joseph W. Steele, was an experienced blockade-runner whom Taylor would come to admire as "absolutely devoid of fear and as careful as a mother."

As the *Banshee* headed west across the open ocean early in 1863, the crew kept a constant lookout for United States Navy

warships. By then the fast-growing U.S. Navy could spare some vessels from blockade duty along the coast, and these ships had begun stopping and searching neutral vessels thousands of miles from the North American coast to determine whether or not they were blockade-runners.

Such inspections by belligerents were permitted under international law. According to the so-called "doctrine of continuous voyage," the U.S. Navy was authorized to seize a neutral merchantman on mere suspicion that her cargo would ultimately arrive in the South—no matter if her papers claimed a neutral destination. A prize court would then decide whether to condemn the ship or set it free.

The fact that a ship's papers indicated it was headed for Nassau or Bermuda simply added weight to the Yankees' doubts, and doubt turned to incredulity when a merchant captain tried to convince a boarding party that his large cargo of weapons or even luxury goods was consigned to an island with a small and unpretentious population in no need of defense. Still, suspicion was one thing and proof another, and a cool-headed merchant skipper who stood his ground sometimes could win the battle of nerves.

Like many other blockade-runners, Taylor considered the Federal tactics fair play. "If the Americans were stretching the theory of blockade," he wrote, "it was only because we were extending its practice. From the very outset the voyages of these vessels showed them to be guilty, and the most barefaced advocate could hardly have maintained without shame that they were protected by their ostensibly neutral destination, when that destination was a notorious nest of offense like Nassau."

The *Banshee* made Nassau with no interference. There the ship was coaled, provisioned and painted a camouflaging gray for the most dangerous leg of her journey—the run into Wilmington. Trailing tatters of smoke from her two rakish funnels, the *Banshee* slipped out of Nassau on a moonless night and set course northwest.

The most important person on board now was a new man named Tom Burroughs, the

Long, low and slender, the blockade-runner *Denbigh* knifes through the waves, her deck crammed with bales of cotton. Repeatedly dodging blockaders between Galveston, Texas, and Cuba, she made such regular trips that Confederates called her "the packet."

coast pilot whom Taylor's agents had recruited in Wilmington. Burroughs' role was to guide the *Banshee* to New Inlet at the mouth of the Cape Fear River in the darkness without running aground—or into a Yankee gunboat. Experience was his only guide: The coast was so low and devoid of landmarks that the only visible sign of it would be the dim white line of surf.

On the third day out, the *Banshee* began her run into Wilmington. After steaming 20 miles north of Cape Fear, Captain Steele rounded the northern flank of the Federal cordon; the *Banshee* crept cautiously down the coast toward New Inlet and sanctuary. "Now the real excitement began," Taylor later recalled. "Hunting, pig-sticking, steeple-chasing, big-game shooting, polo—I have done a little of each—all have their thrilling moments, but none can approach running a blockade."

The night was clear and calm—dangerous conditions for a runner. No lights were allowed to show aboard the *Banshee,* not even the glow of a cigar. The engine-room hatchways were covered with tarpaulins at the risk of suffocating the stokers, and even the tiny light in the compass housing was shielded. Orders were passed in whispers, and except for the dull throbbing of the engines and the soft slop of the paddle blades—which sounded deafening to the jittery crewmen—the *Banshee* steamed on in silence.

The men on deck crouched behind the bulwarks, expecting at any moment to be challenged by a Yankee gunboat. Taylor, Steele and Burroughs stayed on the bridge, eyes straining in the darkness. Periodically, Burroughs requested a sounding, the ship slowed and stopped, and a shadowy figure in the fore-chains heaved the lead and report-

ed the depth and condition of the bottom. The readings were guideposts in Burroughs' mind, and they prompted adjustments in the *Banshee's* course.

As the ship cut through the darkness, Taylor suddenly felt Burroughs' fingers digging into his arm. "There's one of them, Mr. Taylor!" he whispered. "On the starboard bow." Taylor peered into the gloom but saw nothing. Then he heard Steele's reassuring voice. "All right, Burroughs, I see her. Starboard a little. Steady."

A moment later, Taylor made out the black, motionless bulk of a gunboat on the *Banshee's* starboard side. He held his breath, expecting the red flash of a Yankee gun and the roar of an explosion. But the *Banshee* passed unnoticed within 100 feet of the foe. Taylor had just begun to breathe freely again when the pilot whispered, "Steamer on the port bow!"

"Hard aport," muttered Steele, and the *Banshee* again crept by unobserved. But soon another cruiser appeared out of the night, steaming slowly across the blockade-runner's bow. "Stop her," ordered Steele, and the *Banshee* lay dead in the water as the enemy vessel glided past.

Darkness had shielded the *Banshee* but the night was fading fast. The fears of those on board mounted as dawn began to brighten the eastern sky. Where was Fort Fisher? "Still we could not tell where we were," Taylor recalled. "The only thing to do was to creep down along the surf as close in and as fast as we dared. It was a great relief when we suddenly heard Burroughs say, 'It's all right, I see the Big Hill.'"

The Big Hill was little more than a bump on the otherwise flat coastline, but to the experienced eye its presence announced that

The crippled blockade-runner *Lilian* *(center)*, en route from Wilmington to Bermuda with 1,200 bales of cotton, prepares to surrender to pursuing Federal warships on the 24th of August, 1864. Like many other captured runners, the *Lilian* was turned into a blockading ship.

Fort Fisher was very near. And none too soon, for dawn had exposed the *Banshee*. "Six or seven gunboats steamed rapidly towards us and angrily opened fire," Taylor wrote. "Their shots were soon dropping close around us.

"It began to look ugly, when all at once there was a flash from the shore followed by a sound that came like music to our ears—that of a shell whirring over our heads. It was Fort Fisher, wide awake and warning the gunboats to keep their distance. With a parting broadside they steamed sulkily out of range, and in half an hour we were safely over the bar. A boat put off from the fort and then—well, it was the days of champagne cocktails—and one did not run a blockade every day."

Thomas Taylor made seven more trips from Nassau or Bermuda, and he went on to manage his company's blockade-running fleet. The *Banshee* was captured on her ninth run in November of 1863 by U.S. Navy blockaders, condemned, and transformed into a Federal blockade ship herself. By then, however, she had returned a 700 per cent profit to her English owners, and a *Banshee No. 2* had been constructed to join the firm's fleet of runners.

Whenever possible, the English firms recruited their captains from among Royal Navy officers, young men bred to adventure, generally rich in connections but poor in pocket. For them, the American Civil War came as a godsend. A good word here and there secured them long leaves at half pay, and they signed on with firms such as Alexander Collie & Company or the Confederate Trading Company to carry their cargoes through the blockade. The officers used false foreign identities, for the Foreign Enlistment Act enjoined British subjects from engaging in activities on behalf of an alien belligerent.

The chance for wealth made it worth all risks. A captain could expect a salary of $5,000 in gold for a single round trip between Nassau or St. George and the Southern ports. Lower rankings were paid commensurate salaries: The chief engineer got $2,500, the first officer $1,250, and each member of the crew $250. Pilots recruited in Wilmington or Charleston received $3,750 for each round trip. As the War progressed, however, and many pilots were captured (unlike foreign crews, Southerners were never released), experienced pilots came to be in such short supply that they could dictate their own fees.

The greatest profits for captains and officers came not from salaries but from private cargoes that they carried in space allotted them by the owners. Augustus Charles Hobart-Hampden, captain of the blockade-runner *Don*, once visited a Glasgow emporium and purchased 1,000 pairs of corset stays, a large supply of toothbrushes and 500 boxes of Cockle pills, a patent medicine advertised as a cure for liver ailments. He disposed of the corset stays several weeks later in Wilmington, realizing a profit of 1,100 per cent on the transaction; the toothbrushes brought him almost as much in Richmond. Hobart-Hampden was disappointed to discover that there was no market for Cockle pills in Wilmington, but while trying to sell

them he did learn that the South was in desperate need of coffin nails, and he made a mental note to bring in a goodly supply of them on his next voyage.

Hobart-Hampden loaded his ship with cotton for the return trip to Nassau. Worth eight or nine cents a pound on the docks of Wilmington, cotton was bringing 10 times that much in England, and the *Don*, like every other outward-bound blockade-runner, was loaded with cotton to the gunwales. Special steam-powered machinery on the waterfront was used to pack it tightly into bales so that not an inch of space was wasted. The bales were piled so high on the *Don's* decks that the seamen had to stand on them to work the ship. A few more bales were shoehorned into the captain's and officers' cabins as their private cargo.

Hobart-Hampden barely had room in his private storage space for all the boxes of Cockle pills; he now hoped to sell the pills in Nassau, "where everyone," he wrote in his memoirs, "was bilious from overeating and drinking on the strength of the fortunes they were making by blockade-running." The captain's hunch was correct, for in Nassau he found an enterprising druggist willing to make a trade: "He gave me two chests of matches in exchange for my Cockles," Hobart-Hampden recalled, "which matches I ultimately sold in the Confederacy for a very high profit."

Blockade-running also showered sudden riches on the merchants and tradespeople of Bermuda and Nassau. On the streets of St. George and Nassau, blockade-runners, Yankee sailors on shore leave, prostitutes, confidence men and cardsharps rubbed shoulders and spent gold coins with kingly profligacy. A sense of desperate *joie de vivre* infect-

The remains of a blockade-runni side-wheeler rot in the shallows ne Sullivan's Island, South Caroli Many a Confederate captain about be captured wrecked and burn his vessel so that neither ship cargo would fall into Federal han

ed the captains and mates of the blockade-runners. "They were a reckless lot," observed a Confederate midshipman named James Morgan, "and believed in eating, drinking and being merry for fear that they would die on the morrow. Their orgies reminded me of the stories of the pirates in the West Indies.

"They seemed to suffer from a chronic thirst that could only be assuaged by champagne, and one of their amusements was to sit in the windows with bags of shillings and throw handfuls of the coins to a crowd of loafers in the street to see them scramble. It is a singular fact that five years after the War not one of these men had a dollar to bless himself with."

Because of the dependence on Southern trade, sympathy for the Confederacy naturally ran strong in the islands. So intense was the hatred toward Northerners in St. George that the Union consul there was once mobbed in the street. No less emphatic in their pro-Southern views were the British blockade-running captains. They cheered each Southern victory and mourned each Confederate defeat, but their deepest sentiments were summed up in a toast common in the island taverns: "Here's to the Confederates that produce the cotton; to the Yankees that maintain the blockade and keep up the price of cotton; and to the Britishers who buy the cotton and pay the high price for it. So three cheers to a long continuance of the War, and success to blockade-runners!"

Through most of the War, the Confederate government, consistent with its belief in states' rights, made no attempts to control the imports and exports passing through the blockade. Entrepreneurs were given free rein to bring in luxury goods that found a ready and constant market among the South's aristocrats, who paid in gold to maintain their antebellum life styles. This exchange of cotton for nonessential articles was a constant source of anguish to the Confederate government, and indeed to the majority of Southerners, who became desperate for the necessities of life.

Of four major private shippers, only one ignored the custom of putting profit first. The Southern-owned trading business of Fraser, Trenholm & Company became, during the War, the largest of all blockade-running companies. In the course of the War, the firm owned more than 50 ships; and because its chief officer, George Alfred Trenholm, was above all else a Southern patriot, his ships concentrated on carrying necessities. During the early months of 1863 alone, Trenholm's vessels shipped 18,022 bales of cotton in exchange for quantities of much-needed weapons, munitions, salt, iron and coal. And even though Fraser, Trenholm put patriotism first, its total profits from blockade-running may have been as high as $20 million.

Some of the goods shipped to the South were conspicuously frivolous. One captured blockade-runner was found to be carrying a cargo of caricatures of the despised Union Major General Benjamin F. Butler, items that might well have bolstered morale but certainly would have done nothing for the South's barefooted and ill-armed soldiers. Nor was the Confederacy's President completely guiltless in this regard. Jefferson Davis was pleased when an Arabian thoroughbred horse—a gift from a Middle Eastern potentate—arrived in Richmond for his use, despite the fact that it had taken up pre-

Stevedores on the Nassau waterfront unload cotton bales from blockade-runners. "The wharves of Nassau were always piled high with cotton," a Confederate Navy captain wrote. "The streets were alive with activity during daytime and swarming with drunken revellers by night."

cious cargo space aboard a blockade-runner.

By 1863 food was scarce throughout the South and the trading in luxuries had become a public scandal. Finally, in February of 1864, the Confederate Congress reacted to public pressure and moved to regulate the activities of the blockade-runners. The importation of luxury goods was prohibited and, by executive order of President Davis, 50 per cent of all cargo space on board each blockade-runner was reserved full-time for the use of the government.

The new regulations triggered howls of protest from the state governments, which predictably maintained that these rules violated their sovereign rights. The blockade-running syndicates also determined to defeat Richmond's attempts to control their activi-

ties. For a time, a boycott staged by the blockade-runners threatened to cut the life line between the Confederate ports and the European suppliers.

Jefferson Davis stuck to his new policy, but it was an exercise in futility. In the absence of support from the state governments, the Confederate Congress was powerless to enforce its own legislation. This was quickly recognized by the blockade-running syndicates, which resumed their normal activities while virtually ignoring the import-export regulations.

The Confederacy, then, had to rely on its government blockade-runners for the supplies its soldiers and civilians needed to survive. But in the end the South's meager resources could not build, buy or lease near-

ly enough ships for the job, and only a trickle of necessities arrived aboard Confederate vessels. It was not for lack of effort. Southern naval officers did their patriotic best. John Maffitt brought in countless tons of war matériel to Southern wharves. So did his colleague John Wilkinson, another erstwhile United States Navy officer and master of the steamer *R. E. Lee.*

A British-built side-wheeler, the *R. E. Lee* ran the blockade 21 times in little less than a year, taking about 7,000 bales of cotton out of Charleston and Wilmington and returning from Nassau or St. George with immense supplies of munitions and arms.

Wilkinson always managed to outspeed or outwit his pursuers, but he had plenty of close calls. Once, just after passing Cape Fear on an eastbound trip from Wilmington, Wilkinson's lookout sighted the sloop *Iroquois* under sail and steam bearing down on the *Lee.* Wilkinson, his supply of anthracite coal exhausted, was fueling his boilers with much inferior, soft, smoky coal. Building a full head of steam was impossible; the *Lee* was plodding along, and the sloop was closing on her with every passing minute. In an effort to lighten the ship, Wilkinson jetti-

The captured blockade-runner *R. E. Lee*—assigned to blockade duty as the U.S.S. *Fort Donelson*—undergoes repairs near Norfolk, Virginia, in December 1864. A month later she took part in the Union capture of Fort Fisher, effectively closing the blockade-runners' port of Wilmington, North Carolina.

soned his valuable deck cargo of cotton, but still the *Iroquois* bore down. He maneuvered wildly, to no avail.

Then Wilkinson, desperate for a liberating burst of steam, ordered his engineer to soak some of the remaining cargo of cotton in turpentine—a shipment of 30 or 40 barrels was on board. Fed to the flames, this fuel burned furiously, and all of a sudden the *R. E. Lee* was speeding along at 13.5 knots, holding her own. But the *Iroquois* remained in sight.

The chase was several hours old when at 6 p.m. the *Lee* began to falter once more, the burned cotton having fouled the flues. If the steamer could somehow evade the *Iroquois* for an hour or two longer, until darkness fell, she might get away. Wilkinson had another idea. He directed his engineer to keep up as much steam as possible, but at the same time to add coal dust to the fires to produce smoke—normally the bane of the blockade-runner. Within a short time a dense screen of black smoke hung over the water, and the *Lee*, protected by her vaporous shroud, altered course and steamed off to safety as night came on.

Months later the *Lee* was finally caught. At the time she was under the command of a different captain, and Wilkinson bitterly insisted that her capture was the result of "culpable mismanagement."

Wilkinson and his fellow officers sailed for the Confederacy until there were no ports left open. On the night of January 21, 1865, after a rough passage from Bermuda, Wilkinson, then master of the steamer *Chameleon*, approached New Inlet at the mouth of the Cape Fear River. He had no way of knowing what had happened there while he was at sea. On the 15th of January, Fort Fisher had fallen to a combined Federal sea bombardment and amphibious assault. Wilmington, the last haven for blockade-runners, was now sealed off from the sea. And Charleston, though still in Confederate hands, was too heavily guarded to be of any use to the runners.

Wilkinson suspected nothing as his ship steamed into New Inlet, almost under the guns of Fort Fisher. It was not until the fort failed to respond to his lantern signals that he suspected something was wrong—a doubt that was confirmed by the rapid approach of a pair of Federal gunboats. Wilkinson reversed course and narrowly escaped to the open sea. After recoaling at Nassau, he and a handful of other masters, including John Maffitt, decided to make a run for Charleston. They knew how desperately the Confederate armies needed the provisions in the holds of their vessels. But they found Charleston Harbor impenetrable, and fled in frustration.

Wilkinson and the others knew that the days of blockade-running were over. At the docks of Nassau sat 35 fully laden runners worth $15 million with no port to go to. The provisions in their holds, including 2.5 million pounds of bacon, would never reach the starving Southland. Wilkinson, as he was repulsed from Charleston, sensed that much more than his livelihood was at stake: "As we turned away from the land, our hearts sank within us, while the conviction forced itself upon us that the cause for which so much blood had been shed, so many miseries bravely endured, and so many sacrifices cheerfully made, was about to perish at last."

A Yankee Doctor on Blockade Duty

Doctor Charles Stedman, the Boston physician who served as a ship's surgeon during the War, titled his wartime sketches *Doctor Squillgee's Four Years in the U.S. Navy*. In naval parlance, a squilgee was a squeegee for drying the deck.

Although scores of newspaper artists and photographers followed both of the Armies all through the War, there were no accommodations for the press aboard crowded warships. So it was that Doctor Charles Ellery Stedman, a talented amateur draftsman who served aboard three U.S. Navy vessels, became the only artist to cover the naval war on a sustained basis.

Stedman apparently set himself no special task in his drawings. He drew anything that struck his fancy—caricatures of shipmates, amusing vignettes of daily routine, reportorial pictures of fleeing blockade-runners and point-blank duels with Confederate shore batteries. Yet these informal sketches, samples of which are shown on these pages, constitute the most comprehensive eyewitness picture of the war at sea.

Stedman was 30 years old, the scion of a well-to-do Boston family, when he reported for duty aboard the U.S.S. *Huron* on January 8, 1862. The doctor quickly lost any and all illusions of the romance of Navy service.

The shipboard food was abominable, consisting mainly of two vile dishes that the crew called "salt horse" (preserved beef) and "dogs' bodies" (dried peas boiled in a cloth). And the captain, Lieutenant John Downes, was irascible and demanding—a stickler for discipline and a tiger for drill.

During the *Huron's* shakedown cruise in New England waters, the crew was piped, drummed and bugled through lengthy and exhausting practice sessions. There were gunnery drills, fire drills, explosion drills, abandon-ship drills—and then more of the same. Stedman took part in the exercises. Forced to improvise in the *Huron's* cramped quarters, he and his assistants set up their clinic in the officers' wardroom and performed simulated operations on the dining table. The dreary drilling continued until February 5. Then, to the great relief of Stedman and his shipmates, captain Downes concluded the practice cruise and headed south for blockade duty off the Southern coast.

Feeling distinctly seasick, Surgeon Stedman keeps careful hold of a washbasin as his cabin rolls with the ocean's swells. Stedman captioned this drawing, "He wishes he had joined the Army."

Stedman's first ship, the four-gun U.S.S. *Huron*, lies in wait for blockade-runners in the Stono River south of Charleston. The *Huron's* 11-inch Dahlgren, called "Brother Ephraim" by the crew, protrudes to the right of her smokestack.

Stamping and gesturing in a comical rage, captain John Downes of the *Huron* berates a sailor for spitting on the quarterdeck. The captain, wrote Stedman wryly in his picture caption, "is expressing his disapproval."

During a ship-wide practice drill, a gun crew prepares to fire a blank from a Dahlgren cannon.

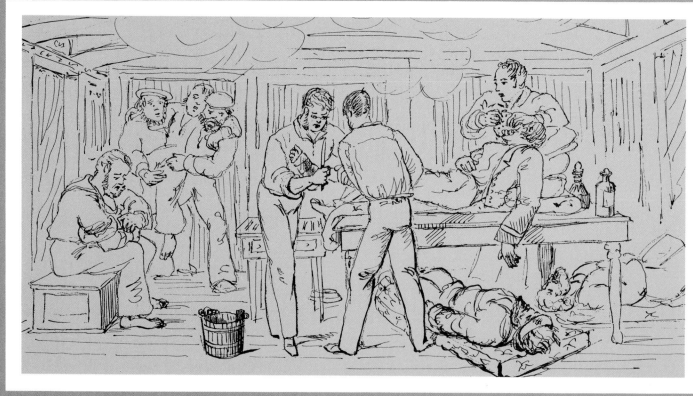

Joining the drill in the *Huron's* wardroom, Surgeon Stedman and his assistants pretend to operate on one of the simulated casualties.

During an off-duty interlude, the chief engineer plays his flute. Most of the sailors spent their free time writing letters, playing cards or reading.

Sailors line up for their last ration of grog in September of 1862. The United States Navy had joined the temperance movement to improve efficiency.

Climaxing a long chase, the U.S.S. *Huron* (*left*) captures the blockade-runner *Cambria* off the coast of South Carolina.

Aboard the *Huron*, the ship's officers *(left)* size up British passengers from the *Cambria*.

An Embarrassing Accident, a Profitable Prize

Stedman's fellow crewmen on board the U.S.S. *Huron* greeted their assignment to the South Atlantic Blockading Squadron with eager anticipation. The squadron's zone of operations—from northern South Carolina to the southern tip of Florida—included Charleston, Savannah and several smaller prime ports for blockade-runners, and everyone expected good hunting and plenty of money for the captured vessels.

Stedman and his shipmates soon found out that it was not at all easy to capture prizes along a coast that their quarry knew much better than they did. On the night of February 10, 1862, off North Carolina, the *Huron* pursued a clever blockade-runner too far inshore—and ran aground off Cape Fear. It took two full days for the men to free the *Huron*, and all the while they expected to be attacked by Confederates from the shore. "To be 48 hours ashore on a hostile coast, with a prospect of a South Easter coming on and everything failing you as you tried your best to get off, is no joker," Sted-

man wrote following this ordeal. "I am about done up with fatigue, want of sleep, excitement and suspense."

But the crew learned quickly, and they put their new skills to good use. On the 26th of May, just before daybreak, lookouts spotted a long, lean steamer about to enter Charleston Harbor. Firing her Parrott rifle, the *Huron* pursued the stranger into the open sea. Four hours later, the British blockade-runner *Cambria* hauled in her sails and surrendered *(opposite page)*. To the delight of the *Huron's* crew, the *Cambria* turned out to be transporting rifles, saltpeter, muslin and medicines—more than enough contraband to make her a valuable prize.

By the autumn of 1862, the *Huron* was badly in need of repairs, and many of her crew—including Stedman—had been stricken with malaria and typhoid. The ship was ordered back to Boston for repairs and "decontamination," and the doctor happily spent several weeks at home.

107

A Sweltering Stint in a Leaky Monitor

Stedman's next ship, the ironclad *Nahant*, was a constant trial and tribulation. Like other ships of the shallow-draft, underpowered monitor type, she proved so unstable that she wallowed and leaked when she took to the open sea. Her metal hull became a veritable frying pan under the broiling Southern sun.

One of the *Nahant*'s duties was to guard the wooden blockading warships against any attacks by Confederate ironclads. And she repeatedly battered the coastal defenses near Charleston and provided close support for subsequent infantry assaults. Stedman came to respect the *Nahant* and the other ironclads for their destructive power in

The *Nahant (center)* and another Union monitor, the *Weehawken (left)*, capture the Confederate ironclad *Atlanta* in Wassaw Sound, Georgia, in June of 1863.

these assignments. "When the monitors opened with their flanking fire," wrote Stedman with pride, "it was too much for Johnny Secesh."

Before long, the *Nahant*'s stifling heat and poor ventilation took their toll on Stedman's health. Again incapacitated by fever, he spent the winter ashore.

Peering through a peephole in the *Nahant*'s cramped turret, the ship's executive officer (*far right*) motions the gunner to adjust his 15-inch cannon and calls out the range.

A member of the *Nahant*'s powder division grapples a cannonball weighing more than 400 pounds. Other crewmen move cartons of powder bags onto a hoist (*far right*) to feed the ship's guns.

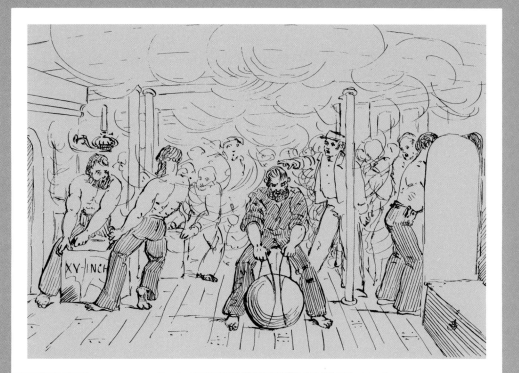

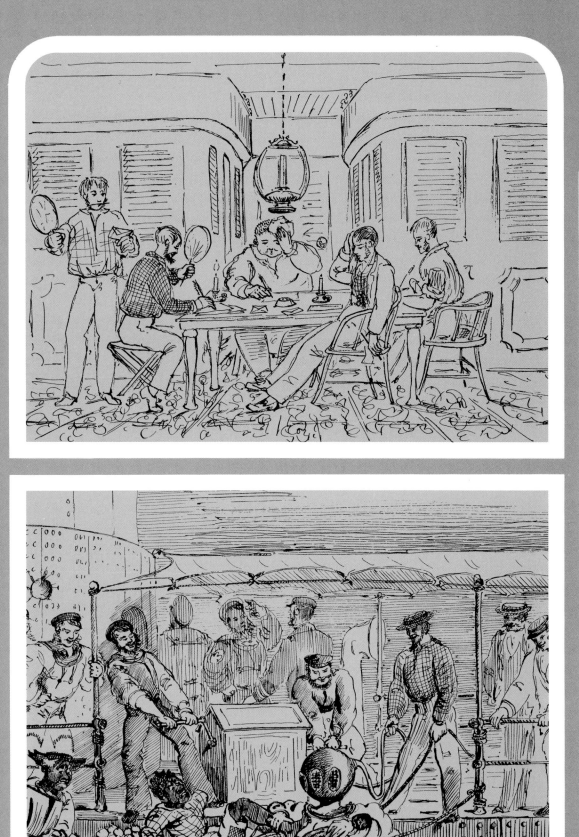

Sweltering below the sun-heated iron deck, Stedman and other officers struggle to write letters. In a note to his wife, Stedman complained, "How can I write all I want to, in a temperature of 98°?"

A diver, surfacing after scraping the *Nahant's* bottom, frightens two freed slaves selling provisions. The bottom had to be cleaned often to rid it of speed-reducing marine growth.

Navy longboats, pitching and tossing in choppy seas, take aboard supplies from Stedman's *Circassian (left)* and deliver the goods to U.S. vessels on blockade duty in the background.

Ferrying Supplies to the Blockaders

In 1864, Stedman was reassigned to the steamer *Circassian*, a captured blockade-runner that had been converted into a U.S. Navy supply ship. From Boston harbor, the *Circassian* ferried ammunition and provisions to blockading ships as far away as Galveston, Texas. The round trips lasted a month and more, and were not particularly eventful. But between them Stedman was able to see his wife and son. As welcome as these visits were, they made Stedman increasingly homesick and vexatious. "I wish I had nothing to do but to be at home," he wrote to his wife, "earning my bread and

On a heaving deck in a raging gale, Surgeon Stedman applies his heel to reset a sailor's dislocated shoulder. Even though the supply ship rarely saw action, her crewmen frequently suffered injuries.

Obeying a bosun's mate's piped order to weigh anchor for the voyage home, crewmen of the *Circassian* turn the spoked capstan that winds up the anchor chain. A fiddler plays a gay chantey to speed the work along.

butter among people that I care about and who care for me.''

Finally, the surgeon got his wish: The War ended, and Stedman returned to Boston for good. There he resumed his medical practice and rendered his shipboard sketches into finished drawings.

Fighting the Secret War

"The most important duty of the diplomatic representatives of the United States in Europe will be to counteract by all proper means the efforts of the agents of that projected Confederacy."

WILLIAM H. SEWARD, UNITED STATES SECRETARY OF STATE, MARCH 26, 1861

On the morning of June 5, 1861, a stout, dignified man with muttonchop whiskers appeared in a staid office hard by the swarming docks and noisy shipyards of Liverpool. He was James Dunwody Bulloch, a Confederate Navy agent on a ship-buying mission, and the business firm was Fraser, Trenholm & Company, the Confederacy's financial agent in Europe. With funds to be forwarded from Richmond to Fraser, Trenholm, Bulloch had been charged to create a Confederate Navy truly worrisome to the North.

Bulloch was one of a few dozen men who would soon figure as principals in a desperate offstage struggle to influence European policy toward the War and obtain material and moral support. Among the fighters in this clandestine battle were diplomats, spies, propagandists and informers. Their activities, carefully hidden from the public eye but occasionally erupting in headlined successes and failures, periodically affected the very conduct of the War. Young Henry Adams, who was serving in London as private secretary to his father, United States Minister to England Charles Francis Adams, felt with reason that the pursuit of victory in Europe was almost as important to the Union cause as the maneuvers of warships on the oceans and armies in the field.

Though the public rarely caught a glimpse of the furtive struggles, participants on both sides found it hard to keep secrets from each other. The War had barely begun on American shores when the United States Legation in London received word of suspicious activity in Liverpool, a likely source of ships for the Confederacy. Benjamin Moran, the waspish Secretary of the U.S. Legation, remarked grimly in his journal, "If this be true, there will be some hanging soon."

But Moran and other Union operatives were to learn soon enough that it was easier to detect ships being built for the Confederacy than it was to prevent their delivery. The British Foreign Enlistment Act of 1819 prohibited the outfitting of warships by belligerents in ports of the home islands or the colonies. However, the Act did not forbid the building of vessels that might become ships of war, so long as they were not armed or supplied with ammunition in Britain. Capitalizing on this loophole, Bulloch went shopping for ships that, with the addition of armament, could be transformed into commerce raiders.

As a former Navy officer, Bulloch knew precisely what he was looking for in a vessel. An essential ingredient was speed, but in addition he wanted ships with large coal capacities and excellent sailing qualities so that they could remain at sea for long periods. He found no such ships available in Britain, so he contracted with local shipyards to build two raiders to his own specifications.

Of course Bulloch took pains to conceal his activities. But to his "utmost astonishment and chagrin," he discovered a complete account of his mission in a copy of *The*

James Bulloch, the Confederacy's chief naval purchasing agent in Europe, was a man of sterling honor. As the captain of a commercial steamer at the start of the War, he went out of his way to return the vessel to her owners in New York before "going South."

New York Times even before he got properly to work. It was clear, as the London *Chronicle* soon observed, that "a system of espionage of the most extensive and searching character has been for some time going on in England." Bulloch's amazement persisted. He informed Richmond that the Union spy apparatus in Europe was so extensive as to be "scarcely credible," that "the servants of gentlemen supposed to have Southern sympathies are tampered with," and that "confidential clerks, and even the messengers from telegraph offices, are bribed to betray their trust."

These shadowy undertakings were largely conceived and personally superintended by Henry Shelton Sanford, the United States Minister in Belgium, who doubled as chief of Federal secret-service operations in Europe. A bright, resourceful and sometimes officious career diplomat, Sanford spent more of his time bustling about Europe to organize espionage activities than he did in the legation at Brussels. In the process he managed to offend many people, including Benjamin Moran, who criticized his "bouncing, ill-mannered" style.

Taking with utmost seriousness a directive from Secretary of State William H. Seward that placed opposition to Confederate agents first on the list of diplomatic priorities, Sanford infiltrated his men into ports, shipyards, mills, factories, and postal and telegraph offices. He suggested bribing a clerk at Lloyd's of London to keep him informed of the sailing of all vessels bound for Confederate ports. If consuls or police agents could find no evidence for seizure, and if clever lawyers were unable to delay the sailings, said Sanford, the ships could be sunk before they got out of the English Channel—

"Accidents are so numerous in the Channel, you know"—or captured at sea by bribed crew members. Ships that managed to escape to the high seas were minutely described, along with their cargoes and dates of departure, in a "black list" that Sanford sent regularly to the commanders of the Federal blockading squadrons.

Sanford held that Bulloch was by all odds "the most dangerous man" the Confederacy had in England. "So dangerous do I consider this man," he wrote, "that I feel disposed when he comes to the Continent to have him arrested on some charge or other." Meantime, he hired a private detective agency headed by an investigator named Ignatius Pollaky to keep a constant watch on Bulloch and other Confederate agents.

Sanford's immediate concern in the summer of 1861 was the construction of a trim, bark-rigged steamer with raked masts and funnels. The new ship, given the cover name *Oreto*, was purportedly on order from the Italian government for service out of Palermo. But Sanford was not deceived. In a letter to Seward in July he warned that the *Oreto* was being built for the Confederacy, and that if the vessel slipped away unhindered she would "do us an infinite deal of mischief."

Sanford was planning how to stop the *Oreto* when he received word from Pollaky that detectives had traced shipments of gun crates from warehouses in London to the distant Scottish port of Greenock. There they found the steamer *Fingal*, recently purchased by Bulloch and preparing to set sail under the British flag. She was loading with 13,000 Enfield rifles, 400 barrels of gunpowder, assorted artillery pieces, medical supplies and vast quantities of British-made Confederate uniforms—perhaps the largest shipment of war matériel ever consigned to the Confederacy.

Speaking on behalf of the United States, Minister Charles Francis Adams officially protested the transparent fiction that the *Fingal* was a British vessel enjoying the protection of the British flag. But Benjamin Moran predicted, correctly, that "this Government won't stop her."

Although the ship was listed as having a British captain, Pollaky assumed correctly that the real commander after she put to sea would be Bulloch himself. On the supposition that she would be ready to sail when Bulloch went aboard, detectives were assigned to watch the ship constantly. But Bulloch eluded them, slipping down the coast and boarding the *Fingal* at Holyhead. He was well out to sea before Pollaky and his men knew he was gone.

Disturbing though it was for the Union, the *Fingal's* escape was soon overshadowed by another blunder that brought the Federal states and Britain perilously close to war. It all began in the autumn of 1861. President Jefferson Davis, dissatisfied with the European performance of his envoys Yancey, Mann and Rost, decided to replace them with two former U.S. Senators—James M. Mason of Virginia and John Slidell of Louisiana. The two were well-known veterans of Southern politics, and it was feared in the North that their appointment, together with the obvious weakness of the blockade and the poor performance of Union armies thus far, might make the European powers more receptive to deals with the Confederacy. A recent visit to Richmond by Sir James Ferguson, a British Member of Parliament, was thought to be a possible prelude to the breaking of the blockade by the British fleet. Un-

der these tense circumstances, U.S. Navy officers were strongly in favor of seizing the envoys at sea.

On the black and rainy night of October 12, Mason and Slidell ran the blockade at Charleston in order to reach Cuba. At Havana, they booked passage for London under protection of the neutral flag of the British mail steamer *Trent*.

The United States consul in Havana had learned of the presence of the Confederate envoys and had informed Washington. A week later, the consul sent a message revealing that Mason and Slidell would embark on the *Trent* on the 7th of November. How, if at all, Washington reacted to this intelligence remains unclear. But Captain Charles Wilkes, the hotheaded and often erratic commander of the U.S. frigate *San Jacinto*, arrived in Havana from the African coast at the end of October and soon afterward intercepted the *Trent* in the Old Bahama Channel, 300 miles to the east. Wilkes dispatched a boarding party and forcibly removed Mason and Slidell before permitting the *Trent* to continue on her way.

The seizure was greeted with outrage in the South—Jefferson Davis said it violated rights of embassy "held sacred even amongst barbarians"—and with enormous enthusiasm in the North. When Wilkes arrived in Boston to deposit his prisoners at Fort Warren, he was acclaimed a hero. His action, said the Boston *Transcript*, was "one of those bold strokes by which the destinies of nations are determined." "Let us stand by the act of Wilkes," said the Milwaukee *Morning Sentinel*, "though all the guns of Europe frown on us." *The New York Times* suggested that a second Fourth of July be proclaimed in Wilkes's honor. The U.S. House

The ironclad *Atlanta*, rebuilt in Savannah from the blockade-runner *Fingal*, lies in a Pennsylvania shipyard, destined for scrap. In her first clash as a Confederate warship she ran aground under the weight of her new armament, was captured by a Federal monitor and pressed into duty with the blockading fleet.

of Representatives gave him an official vote of gratitude and a gold medal, and Navy Secretary Welles wrote to Wilkes that his "great public service" had "the emphatic approval of this Department."

Yet thoughtful people, in and out of government, felt that Wilkes had acted hastily and perhaps unwisely. He had an indisputable right under international law to stop a neutral vessel suspected of carrying contraband. But could envoys be considered legal prizes of war? And even if they could be, Wilkes clearly had no authority to adjudicate the question on the spot by seizing the Confederate envoys and then permitting the *Trent* to continue her voyage. The proper course would have been to take the *Trent* into port, where a prize court could hand down a verdict.

Bucking public sentiment, Charles Sumner, Chairman of the Senate Foreign Relations Committee, urged the immediate release of the diplomats to forestall a break

in relations—or even war—with Britain. President Lincoln himself admitted that Mason and Slidell might "prove to be white elephants." That they were: Britain's reaction, when it came, was sheer fury. "You may stand for this," Prime Minister Lord Palmerston told his Cabinet, "but damned if I will!" War fever swept the nation. "In one month," said the London *Morning Post,* "we could sweep all the *San Jacintos* from the seas, blockade the Northern ports and turn to a direct and speedy issue the war." Further inflaming the public was a false story that had the mail agent of the *Trent* stepping between Slidell's young daughter and the bayonets of the boarding party with the words, "Back, you poltroons!"

Benjamin Moran noted that the *Trent* Affair would "do more for the Southerners than 10 victories, for it touches John Bull's honor, and the honor of his flag." Moran was convinced that "nothing but a miracle" could prevent Lord Palmerston from "getting up a war." Mrs. Charles Francis Adams and Lady Palmerston, he added dryly, had "a crying match" over the terrifying prospect. Britain's Royal Navy went on alert and 11,000 British troops sailed for Canada, leading Henry Adams to write, "This nation means to make war. Do not doubt it."

The anger of the British government was fed by a conviction that U.S. Secretary of State Seward was profoundly anti-British. *The Times* of London reflected government opinion when it editorialized that "the splenetic mind of Mr. Seward" wanted a war with Britain as a pretext for seizing Canada in recompense for the loss of the South. British Foreign Secretary Lord John Russell wrote to the British Minister to the United States, Lord Richard Lyons, "The best thing would be if Seward could be turned out, and a rational man put in his place." Lyons himself reported to London that he had learned from private sources that Seward had signed the orders for the seizure of the *Trent* "without the knowledge of the President."

British fears and suspicions were not totally unfounded. Seward was indeed skeptical of England's motives. He believed that the English were happy to see as powerful a trade rival as the United States divided and weakened, and he did not rule out British intervention to make the division permanent. From time to time he made bellicose threats to break off relations with the British if they so much as talked to representatives of the Confederacy.

In this tense situation the United States was fortunate to have as its Minister in London Charles Francis Adams, who happened to be the son and grandson of American Presidents. Although Adams was not brilliant or exceptionally imaginative, he did possess iron restraint and an extraordinary capacity for making cool judgments under pressure. When he was confronted with a crisis, according to son Henry, "not a word escaped, not a nerve twitched."

The Minister used all his poise when he received word of the *Trent* Affair. A telegram was handed to him while he was visiting the Yorkshire country home of a member of Parliament. Although he recognized that it might be "the final calamity in this contest," Adams said not a word and remained a guest through the weekend rather than return to London and face questions there before additional information could arrive from Washington.

When he returned to the legation, Adams worked tirelessly and effectively to cool tempers on both sides. The very slowness of communications helped to keep the dispute from flaring into war: Though a transatlantic cable had been laid in 1858, it was out of commission, and the 14 days or so that a message took to cross the ocean by ship gave both sides time to reflect.

Reflection revealed that neither nation wanted war. The United States had one on its hands already and wished to avoid another. Great Britain had its position in the world to consider. As rulers of the world's largest empire, the British were traditionally defenders of the status quo, and reluctant to challenge the legitimacy of any existing government. More important, this was a time when the balance of power in Europe was dangerously unstable. Italy was emerging as a unified nation after decades of struggle. In Poland, an insurrection was brewing against the country's czarist Russian masters. An Austro-Prussian war loomed, and France and Russia were dangerously aroused over the growing British influence in Greece and the eastern Mediterranean. It was scarcely the moment, in Lord Palmerston's view, to commit Great Britain to a risky adventure in far-off America.

Since neither Britain nor the United States wanted war, there was none. Queen Victoria's consort, Prince Albert, prepared a carefully worded note giving the United States government the opportunity to save face by disclaiming Wilkes's action on the grounds that it was unauthorized. The Lincoln Cabinet accepted this compromise, and Seward wrote to Lord Lyons that the Confederate envoys were being "cheerfully liberated." Although he did not issue an official apology, Seward assured Lord Lyons that Wilkes had indeed acted without authorization. The crisis passed.

After the release of Mason and Slidell on January 1, 1862, tensions subsided for a while. Charles Francis Adams confided to a friend that for the first time he felt justified in signing a lease for a London house for more than one month at a time.

For the Confederates, the affair was a distinct setback if only because it failed to bring any of the concrete British help that it had seemed certain to produce. This was an occa-

In a cartoon published in New York at the height of the *Trent* Affair, U.S. Secretary of State Seward *(beside the American eagle)* returns the hijacked Confederate commissioners Slidell and Mason *(in boat)* to Europe. His act appeases Lord Russell *(foot on the British lion)* but frustrates Jefferson Davis *(far right)*, who had hoped that an incensed England would enter the War as an ally of the South.

sion for the Confederates to reevaluate their efforts to win British support. An energetic propaganda campaign was now launched under the direction of a 27-year-old Alabamian of Swiss birth named Henry Hotze, who arrived in London just as the *Trent* Affair was being resolved.

Hotze was concerned that the British public was dependent on the "mendacious" Northern press for its view of America. He therefore decided to publish a roundup of news and opinion that he called the *Index: A Weekly Journal of Politics, Literature and News*. As a skilled propagandist, he knew that his best weapon was a reputation for reliability, and the *Index* quickly became a primary source of accurate war news with a Southern slant. Some of the leading English journalists wrote for the paper, and they carried their pro-Southern views to the journals and newspapers for which they normally wrote, thus giving Hotze "the opportunity of multiplying myself, so to speak, to an almost unlimited extent." For that reason—and because the *Index* readership included most of England's important editors, politicians and Cabinet ministers—the paper had an influence far beyond its circulation, which never climbed above 2,250.

Southern propaganda in France was in the hands of Edwin De Leon, a well-connected South Carolina journalist and diplomat. Although Napoleon III was sympathetic to the Confederate cause, most of the French people vaguely favored the Union—in part because of the Northern monopoly on war news reaching French newspapers. Nevertheless, De Leon had little trouble bribing the notoriously venal French press, and soon he was able to report that more than 200 newspapers were carrying articles either supplied by him directly or written by French journalists in his pay.

But De Leon had a falling-out with Slidell and was dismissed. Hotze took over French as well as British propaganda. Confederate funds were by this time running so low that Hotze was unable to keep on bribing the French press, as De Leon had done. Instead, he cultivated an acquaintance with Auguste Havas, director of the Havas-Bullier Telegraphic and Correspondence Agency, whose *Blue Sheet* enjoyed a virtual monopoly on French translations of news from abroad. He sold Havas on the idea that he could furnish more reliable war news than could be obtained from any of the Northern newspapers or agencies. Using Havas as a conduit, Hotze was henceforth able to dictate the war coverage of three quarters of the French press.

Among Hotze's prime objectives was to convince foreigners that the Confederacy was firmly established as an independent nation, with all the rights of commerce that such sovereignty implied. Acceptance of that idea would be of great aid to Confederate purchasing agents, who needed all the help they could get to counteract the doubts and suspicions aroused by the *Trent* Affair.

In the interim, tensions were building again—this time over the Confederate commerce raiders under construction in British yards. After delivering the *Fingal* and its cargo to Savannah in November 1861, James Bulloch returned to England to oversee the construction of the *Oreto* and of a second steamer that was known as the *No. 290* and then, when launched, as the *Enrica*. Thomas H. Dudley, the aggressive American consul in Liverpool, discovered that funds to pay for the *Oreto's* engines had come from Fraser, Trenholm & Company—already wide-

PUNCH, OR THE LONDON CHARIVARI.—August 27, 1864.

AMERICA
ANOTHER FEDERAL
DEFEAT

VERY PROBABLE.

Lord Punch. "THAT WAS JEFF DAVIS, PAM! DON'T YOU RECOGNISE HIM?"
Lord Pam. "HM! WELL, NOT EXACTLY—MAY HAVE TO DO SO SOME OF THESE DAYS."

ly recognized as agents of the Confederacy.

Dudley passed his information to Minister Charles Francis Adams, who presented the Foreign Office with a protest against violations of neutrality. But Dudley and Adams met with obdurate Foreign Office bureaucrats, who struck Henry Adams as "discourteous in their indifference and insolent in their disregard of truth." At this point, in mid-1862, Confederate armies had won a significant victory in the Second Battle of Bull Run, and Britain's Foreign Minister, Lord Russell, reflected the growing belief within the Cabinet that the Confederate States were very likely to win the American Civil War. Indeed, Russell and Palmerston were waiting only for a sufficiently decisive Confederate victory to recognize the Confederacy as an independent nation. Under the circumstances, it was important not to antagonize Southern opinion by too scrupulous an interpretation of the meaning of neutrality and the letter of the Foreign Enlistment Act.

Russell's reply to the evidence Dudley provided was to send customs officers to examine the *Oreto*. The officers disregarded the gunports cut into the ship's sides, which were in fact legal constructions so long as no guns were installed, and reported that "she had no warlike stores of any kind on board." Under the circumstances, explained Lord Russell, he had no legal grounds for detaining the ship.

It appeared that Bulloch had not permitted any incriminating evidence aboard; he was taking no chances. On March 22, 1862, he invited a group of guests, including a few women, to come aboard the *Oreto* for a trial run. The ship left port under a British flag and a British captain. After cruising around the harbor area, she lowered several small boats and sent the women and all but one of the male guests back to shore. The remaining passenger was John Low of the Confederate Navy. The *Oreto* put out to sea headed for Nassau.

Traveling mostly under sail in light winds, the *Oreto* arrived in the Bahamas 37 days later. She made rendezvous at a small island on the edge of the Great Bahama Bank with a schooner loaded with military supplies. The *Oreto* took on ammunition and four 7-inch rifled guns, hoisted the Confederate flag and put out to sea again as the commerce raider *Florida*.

Bulloch now stepped up work on the *No. 290*. Thwarted in their efforts to stop the *Oreto*, Adams and Dudley were determined to prevent the departure of this new ship, which Bulloch correctly judged to be "superior to any vessel of her date in fitness for the purposes of a sea rover." Dudley got an oral statement from the foreman at Laird's ship-yards that the *290* would carry 11 guns. Waterproof ammunition magazines had already been built into her, and platforms had been screwed into her decks for pivot guns. This testimony was dismissed by the Commissioners of Customs in Liverpool as insufficient evidence. Convinced that Liverpool Customs was Confederate oriented, Adams took two additional steps. He asked that the Federal warship *Tuscarora*, which was then in British waters, move into position to intercept the *290* if she should actually put to sea. He then sought an opinion from Robert Porrett Collier, who as Judge Advocate of the British fleet was England's top authority on maritime law.

Collier's reply was unequivocal: There could hardly be a "stronger case of infringement of the Foreign Enlistment Act." Adams took this opinion to Lord Russell, who at last was persuaded to ask the Queen's Advocate, Sir John Harding, to review the case.

In sending the evidence to Harding, Lord Russell stressed that he needed a quick legal opinion. What nobody knew was that Harding had just suffered a suspected stroke. By the time Lord Russell learned that Harding was in no condition to give an opinion, five critical days had elapsed. Lord Russell immediately sent out orders to detain the *290*. But he was too late; she had sailed early on the morning of July 29, 1862, under her other name, the *Enrica*. She was bound for the island of Terceira in the Azores, where she would take on armament and become the legendary raider *Alabama*.

Bulloch's accomplishment in delivering the *Florida* and *Alabama* into Confederate hands was all the more remarkable because he had been forced to operate with scant cash and severely limited lines of credit. The Confederate government, short of gold and silver, relied heavily on bond issues. At first, banks, commercial houses and individuals responded with enthusiasm. But the specie thus obtained was quickly sucked out of the country, going through the Liverpool offices of Fraser, Trenholm, into the hands of Confederate purchasing agents like Bulloch, and eventually into the bank accounts of European suppliers. When voluntary support fell off drastically in the second year of the War, the government began to rely for its operating expenses on paper notes with no gold or silver backing. So rapidly did these notes decline in value that Confederate soldiers were sometimes paid in sounder Northern greenbacks, which were accepted by many Southerners as a subsidiary tender.

To make things even more difficult for the Confederates in Europe, Union operatives spread stories to the effect that the Confederacy and its securities were poor credit risks. Northern purchasing agents, well supplied with Federal gold, endeavored to bid up the cost of war materials so high that the South could not afford them. Thus Henry Sanford bought the entire available European supply of saltpeter, an essential ingredient of gunpowder. When he heard that Confederate agents were about to sign a contract with a Belgian manufacturer for 60,000 rifles, he immediately made a higher bid and secured the guns for the Union. "I hope they will be effective," he wrote, "in destroying the Rebels for whom they were intended."

In desperation, the Confederacy tried to float loans. The most ambitious of these was the Erlanger loan, which grew out of a meeting in Paris between John Slidell and repre-

The ways at Liverpool's Birkenhead shipyard are filled with vessels under construction in this lithograph of the scene in 1862, when the C.S.S. *Alabama* was completed and launched. The largest of the three unfinished hulls is believed to be that of the future commerce raider.

sentatives of Emile Erlanger, head of the most influential banking house in France. Erlanger agreed to a $15 million loan secured by bonds exchangeable for cotton, which would be sold to the bondholders at the unprecedented low price of sixpence—about 12 cents—a pound. Since cotton was then selling for 21 cents a pound on the open market, the margin for profit was enormous. Erlanger insisted on a 5 per cent commission for selling the bonds, along with stiff interest rates. Confederate Secretary of State Judah P. Benjamin thought the terms verged on

extortion, but after obtaining a few minor concessions he approved the loan anyway, hoping that the close ties the bankers were rumored to have with the French court might help tilt the French toward recognizing the Confederacy.

When the bond issue went on sale on March 19, 1863, it was at first heavily oversubscribed. William Gladstone, the British Chancellor of the Exchequer, was among the enthusiastic buyers. But Federal propaganda—together with the Confederate loss of Vicksburg in July—discredited the se-

In Bristol, England, the speedy packet *Old Dominion* is refitted as a blockade-runner for the Confederacy. The local U.S. consul had this picture taken to aid in intercepting the ship once she left port.

curities and caused their market price to drop precipitously. Although British investors lost fortunes, the Erlangers made a handsome six million dollars in interest and commissions, leaving for the Confederate government some nine million dollars in gold-backed British and French currency.

The Confederates were delighted to have this cash coming in, for by early 1863 they were heavily involved in their most ambitious naval purchasing operation of the War. On direct orders from Confederate Navy Secretary Mallory, they were trying to build a force of ironclads that would offset the numerical superiority of the Federal Navy. What was required, said Mallory, was "a few ships that can receive without material injury the fire of the heaviest frigates" while employing "shell or hot shot to destroy the wooden navy of our enemy."

Confederate agents signed contracts with the shipbuilders James and George Thompson of Glasgow, and with John Laird and Sons of Liverpool. The Thompsons were to build an armored frigate of 3,200 tons, while the Lairds were to deliver two ironclads, each equipped with powerful 9-inch rifled guns in turret batteries and long, pointed iron prows or rams to smash holes in the wooden hulls of Union blockaders. Bulloch was personally to supervise the construction of the ironclads, but another Confederate agent, Commander James H. North, was put in charge of the frigate.

From the start, it was impossible to conceal the nature of the vessels: Armed or not, they could be nothing but ships of war. One clause of the Foreign Enlistment Act provided that even if a ship was unarmed, the British government could seize it on the basis of "intent inferred through structure." Bul-

loch was well aware of this, but he also knew that it would be difficult for Minister Adams to get the British government to act. For just as the hulls of the ironclads were beginning to take shape, Britain and France were devoting their most serious consideration to the recognition of the Confederacy.

The failure of the Federal Army in General George B. McClellan's Peninsula Campaign, combined with General Robert E. Lee's victory at the Second Battle of Bull Run and his subsequent invasion of Maryland, convinced Palmerston and Russell that the United States would be hard pressed to subjugate the Confederate States. At the same time, both men were aware that the Lancashire mills were beginning to suffer from the shortage of cotton caused by the blockade. Almost all of the mills were operating on short time, and 330,000 cotton workers—more than half of the industry's work force—were unemployed.

Palmerston wrote Russell that if the Confederates took Washington or Baltimore, as expected, perhaps it would be time for Britain and France to "address the contending parties and recommend an arrangement on the basis of separation." Russell replied that he agreed to mediation "with a view to the recognition of the independence of the Confederates." Going a step further, he added: "In case of failure, we ought ourselves to recognize the Southern States." In France, Napoleon III was thinking along the same lines. He sent a coded message to his Foreign Minister, who was then in London: "Ask the English government if they don't think the time has come to recognize the South."

The issue was scheduled to be discussed at a special meeting of the British Cabinet in late October of 1862. But before then, news arrived of two crucial events: Lee's invasion of Maryland had been stopped at the Battle of Antietam on September 17, and on September 22 Lincoln had issued his preliminary Emancipation Proclamation. Suddenly, British leaders were no longer so confident of Confederate victory. Palmerston wrote to Russell: "We must continue merely to be lookers-on till the war shall have taken a more decided turn."

In fact, the British leadership had little choice: For many, the Emancipation Proclamation turned the War into a crusade for freedom and human rights. Once Lincoln had put the War on that footing, popular sentiment swung so overwhelmingly to the North that no European government could afford to back the Confederacy openly. Henry Adams hardly exaggerated when he wrote that "the Emancipation Proclamation has done more for us than all our former victories and all our diplomacy."

Yet the younger Adams, like his father, would soon discover in the matter of the Laird rams that the British leadership was both unbending and unpredictable. Indeed, the threat to the Union posed by these vessels, and the fear of their imminent departure, precipitated the last great diplomatic crisis of the War.

In January and February of 1863, as work on the rams progressed, the usually optimistic Bulloch became gloomy about his chances of ever delivering them to the Confederacy. "Think British government will prevent iron ships leaving," he said in a cipher dispatch to Navy Secretary Mallory, adding that the purpose of the ships was "too evident for disguise." By June, the Confederate commissioners advised Commander North to try to sell the armored frigate being built by the

Thompsons; North delayed, saying he still had hopes of getting the ship to sea.

Secretary Mallory replied to Bulloch's dispatch by telling him to sell the rams to a French firm, which would be under contract to turn them over to the Confederacy.

Bulloch duly transferred ownership of the rams to Bravay & Company of Paris, purchasing agents, who ostensibly would be buying them for the Pasha of Egypt. Between them, Bulloch and Bravay managed to make the transaction so complex that Federal agents in Britain, France and Egypt were unable to find any documentary proof that the rams were ultimately bound for the Confederacy.

When the first ram was launched on July 4, Bulloch was again in an ebullient mood. There was no reason, he wrote Mallory, why these supposedly invincible ships could not

Lord Richard Lyons, Great Britain's Minister to the United States, was a quiet, earnest bachelor who eschewed smoking and drinking. Yet he was a gracious host, and the small dinner parties that he gave were reported to be among the finest in Washington.

break the blockade, then proceed up the Potomac River to "render Washington untenable" and sail on to Portsmouth, New Hampshire, to destroy the navy yard there. The vessels could then help liberate New Orleans from Union occupation and free the length of the Mississippi River from Federal domination.

Charles Francis Adams, meantime, was engaged in the kind of diplomatic warfare that his son described as "violent pulling, pushing, threatening, shaking, cursing and coaxing." Adams learned in early summer that the first ram was about to be towed to sea to have its turret fitted outside British territorial waters. The second ram, he was told, was about to be completed by workmen laboring overtime under gaslight. Adams wrote a strong note to Russell in which he spoke of the "active malevolence" of the

The U.S. Minister to England, Charles Francis Adams constantly protested the Confederates' purchase of British-built ships. "None of our generals, not Grant himself," wrote poet James Russell Lowell, "did us better or more trying service than he in his forlorn outpost of London."

British government; he warned that failure to seize the rams would be "virtually tantamount to a participation in the war by the people of Great Britain." In his office at the legation, Benjamin Moran fumed about Britain's "bastard neutrality."

Under Adams' constant prodding, Lord Russell grudgingly sent customs officials to examine the rams and question the builders about their ownership. The inspectors gathered much hearsay evidence, according to Russell, but no solid documentation that the rams were bound for the Confederacy. "Under these circumstances," wrote Russell to Adams on September 1, "Her Majesty's Government cannot interfere in any way with these vessels."

To Adams, this seemed like a deliberate refusal to look facts in the face. He composed a tough reply expressing his "profound regret" at the British government's uncooperative attitude and concluding with a sentence that became famous: "It would be superfluous in me to point out to your Lordship that this is war."

Ringing though that declaration was, it had in fact been carefully thought out by Adams to permit a denial of the intent to wage war. Adams meant—or at least could claim to have meant—that England's release of the rams would automatically constitute a de facto state of war between Britain and the United States.

In any case, Russell had decided before the message arrived to withhold the ships from the Confederates. He felt that Britain had no other choice if it did not want to rupture relations and sever lucrative trade ties with the North. On September 3 he ordered the rams to be detained pending further investigation. To reconcile this abrupt change of mind, he insisted that the British government's action was merely "detention" and not "seizure." The British eventually disposed of the rams by buying them from Bravay & Company for service in the Royal Navy. As for Thompson's frigate, Confederate Commander North had finally despaired of getting her to sea and had sold her to the Danes as the *Danmark*.

The loss of the three vessels—fighting ships counted on to turn the tide in the naval war—was a bitter blow to the Confederacy. Bulloch wrote that it caused him "greater pain and regret than I ever thought it possible to feel." Henry Adams was naturally elated: Stopping the rams, he said, was a "second Vicksburg" and "the crowning stroke of our diplomacy."

Yet the Confederate Navy refused to abandon its quest for ironclads. There remained the hope of getting such vessels from France, where the government of Napoleon III had consistently shown itself to be more sympathetic to the Confederacy than any other government of Europe. From the beginning, Napoleon had made it clear that he was prepared to recognize the Confederacy and break the blockade—but not without the backing of the British fleet. In adopting this pro-Confederate position, he was increasingly supported by the French public, which up to the time of Lincoln's Emancipation Proclamation saw the question of freedom as relating not to the slaves but to the South's right to self-determination.

Napoleon's own motives were complex. On one hand, he was worried that if the Union did not survive there would be no effective counterweight to English maritime power, which he feared. On the other hand, he was pleased to see the division and weakening of a formidable trade rival such as the United States. Most important, Napoleon believed the Confederacy would support him in his misguided attempt to increase the imperial glories of France by destroying the Juárez regime in Mexico and establishing a puppet government in violation of the Monroe Doctrine.

None of these motives were finally strong enough to prompt France to intervene without British support—but they were sufficient to keep Napoleon in a fever of indecision: "If the North is victorious I shall be happy," he said. "If the South is victorious, I shall be enchanted." As for the Confederate representatives in France, they were in a constant turmoil of rising and falling expectations.

When Bulloch decided to shop for ironclads in France, he was counting heavily on the good will of the Emperor, and on assurances that the government considered the construction of ironclads for export to be "a legitimate branch of French trade." Confederate Minister Slidell obtained an audience with the Emperor and asked him bluntly if Confederate ironclads built in France would be allowed to put to sea. "You may build the ships," Napoleon replied, "but it will be necessary that their destination be concealed." With money from the Erlanger loan, Bulloch now went ahead and signed two contracts with Lucien Arman, the biggest shipbuilder in France, for the construction of a powerful squadron of four fast steamers and two ironclads.

The shipbuilder got government authorization, and provided the flimsy excuse that the cruisers were bound for the China Sea trade and that the ironclads—provisionally named the *Sphinx* and the *Cheops*—were in-

The *Wivern* (right, top) was one of two ironclads built for the Confederacy by the Laird Company but never delivered because of U.S. diplomatic protest. The working plans for the Laird ships (bottom) included twin gun turrets, iron plating four and one half inches thick, and a bow reinforced with wrought iron for ramming enemy ships.

tended for Egypt. The heavy armament of the cruisers, Arman added blandly, was necessary protection against the pirates roaming the China Sea. The Minister of Marine was content to leave it at that—and would have done so had it not been for an enterprising shipyard clerk named Trémont, who turned up one morning in the Paris office of U.S. Minister William Dayton.

Trémont had with him documents and correspondence showing that the cruisers and ironclads, being built at Bordeaux and Nantes, were intended for the Confederacy. On payment of 15,000 francs ($3,000), Trémont surrendered the documents. Dayton sent copies of the papers, along with a careful note, to the French Foreign Minister, politely requesting that the French government halt construction of the ships.

The government equivocated, unwilling to act without Britain. Napoleon was still convinced in the spring of 1863 that the South had an excellent chance of winning the War. He reasoned that if he waited until the ships were almost ready for launching, he could release or detain them, depending on which side then appeared stronger. Accordingly, work on the ships continued well into the following winter, while Dayton's complaints grew more bitter. But by then Napoleon's enthusiasm for the Confederacy was dwindling. He was particularly shaken by news of the defeat at Gettysburg—and he was anxious to improve his relations with the United States in order to preserve his puppet government in Mexico. Seward was shrewd enough to play on Napoleon's concern to advance the Union position. On the 18th of February, 1864, Bulloch wrote to Mallory that the French government had forbidden the departure of the ironclads and had ordered the sale of the four fast steamers.

The Confederate purchasing agents still had one last, slim hope. The government had urged Arman to sell all the ships to other foreign buyers. Some ships went to Peru and others to Prussia, while Denmark contracted to buy the ironclad *Sphinx*. But once the Danes' war with Prussia ended, they were anxious to divest themselves of the *Sphinx*. The ship reverted to Arman, and Bulloch eventually bought her for the Confederacy. She proved to be sluggish and unseaworthy, but she was commissioned anyway and sent to sea under the Confederate flag, bearing the name *Stonewall*. But the vessel did not reach America until the War was over.

Looking back years later, Bulloch admitted that he had been discouraged from time to time by the results of his work. Certainly he had failed to build a naval force that could openly challenge the Federal Navy. But his efforts were not entirely in vain—as the North discovered when Confederate commerce raiders like the *Florida* and the *Alabama* began roaming the sea lanes in search of prey.

Aflutter with flags, the Russian sloop *Vitiaz* (*left*) lies at anchor in New York. The commander of the six-ship Russian fleet, Admiral Stephan Lisovski (*below*), retained a warm spot in his heart for Americans: He had once been rescued by a U.S. warship after his vessel foundered in a tidal wave off Japan.

The black-hulled Russian Atlantic fleet, lying in the Hudson River, is inspected by curious New Yorkers aboard steam barges, paddle-wheelers and pleasure craft.

A Heartening Visit by the Czar's Fleet

Uninvited and unannounced, the frigate *Osliaba*, flying the ensign of Czar Alexander II's Imperial Russian Navy, sailed into New York Harbor on September 11, 1863. In the next three weeks, the *Osliaba* was joined by five other warships. Among them was the 51-gun frigate *Alexander Nevski*, flagship of the Atlantic fleet commander, Rear Admiral Stephan S. Lisovski.

Northerners rejoiced at the unexpected visit. It seemed to them that the Russian fleet might support the hard-pressed U.S. Navy if—as they perennially feared—the powerful British and French fleets intervened to aid the Confederacy. The Czar was indeed hostile to Britain and France, which threatened him as he suppressed a rebellion in Poland. But it was the Czar's fear of war with England and France, not his sympathy for the Union cause, that had prompted him to send his fleet to safety in U.S. ports.

In any event, the North lionized the Russians, opening with a grand review of the Russian fleet in the Hudson River. As New York officials aboard the steamer *Andrews* neared the *Alexander Nevski*, their shipboard band played "God Save the Emperor." In reply, a band on the *Nevski* played what the Russians thought was the American national hymn: "Yankee Doodle."

The Russians had dropped anchor within eyeshot of some potential enemies: four French and three English warships that happened to be visiting New York at the time.

Escorted by police and cavalrymen, officers of the Russian fleet ride carriages down Broadway to an exuberant welcome from thousands of New Yorkers. The Russians

overcome by the reception, shouted their thanks and doffed their gold-laced hats to the cheering crowds.

Joyful Times, Somber Portraits

After two cold and dreary months at sea, the Russians plunged eagerly into the pleasures of city life. They went sightseeing, sat endlessly for photographs, and patronized restaurants, saloons and brothels. "An extra quantity of wine," confessed a midshipman, "came somehow to be consumed rather often."

The officers were repeatedly entertained at lavish functions. The most elaborate affair was held at the New York Academy of Music. Hundreds of guests feasted on 12,000 oysters, 1,000 pounds of tenderloin, 360 pounds of salmon and 250 turkeys—all of it washed down with 3,500 bottles of wine and champagne.

In the academy's ballroom (*pages 138-139*), bejeweled socialites in voluminous gowns vied to waltz and polka with the Czar's men. But the results were somewhat disappointing to the dancers. Most of the Russians were shorter than the women had expected and, reported the *New York Herald*, they disappeared "in the embrace of grand nebulous masses of muslin and crinoline, whirled hither and thither as if in terrible torment."

Frozen-faced officers of the Russian sloop *Variag* stare out of a formal portrait, giving no hint of the good times they were having.

Posing in Mathew Brady's studio in New York, Admiral Lisovski *(center)* is flanked by the captains of the six visiting Russian vessels.

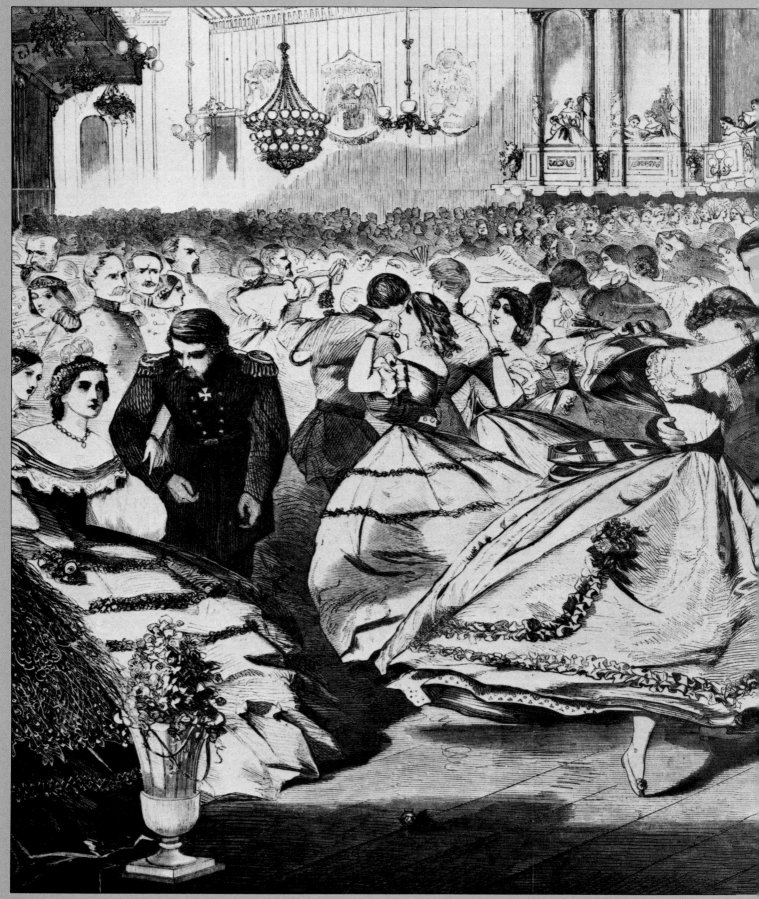

Russian officers, portrayed larger than life by a popularizing artist, waltz their partners at the Great Russian Ball in the Academy of Music. The ball and banque

reportedly cost one million dollars, and many Northerners questioned the propriety of such a gala while Union soldiers were starving and dying in prison camps.

"God Bless the Russians"

From New York, the Russians sailed up and down the East Coast, seeing and being seen in a dozen cities. In Boston, the crew members paraded on Boston Common. In Washington, President Abraham Lincoln entertained the Russians at a White House reception. The grand tour finally ended in April of 1864 when the Czar, no longer worried about a war with England and France, sent his fleet on other missions.

By then, the possibility of European intervention on the Confederate side had also passed. But Northerners were nonetheless grateful for the morale-building visit of their newfound allies from the East. Speaking for his countrymen, U.S. Navy Secretary Gideon Welles declared, "God bless the Russians."

At Battery Rodgers, Virginia, a Russian warship lies in the Potomac River beyond a 15-inch Union cannon.

Sightseeing Russian officers form ranks at Niagara Falls. American guides escorted them free of charge.

Alexandria, crewmen cling to the rigging of the *Osliaba*. From there the Russians visited a Virginia encampment, where they gamely tried to ride U.S. Cavalry horses.

The Depredations of Captain Semmes

"Chasing a sail is very much like pursuing a coy maiden, the very coyness sharpening the pursuit."

CAPTAIN RAPHAEL SEMMES, CONFEDERATE STATES NAVY

5

The Federal officers and sailors on blockade duty off the port of Galveston, Texas, were more than a little anxious on January 11, 1863. Commodore Henry H. Bell, who flew his flag aboard the 21-gun steam sloop *Brooklyn*, had been assigned to capture Galveston. The port had already changed hands twice; a Union landing force had seized it in October 1862, and the Confederates had recaptured it on January 1, 1863. Now Bell, just having failed in an attempt to bombard the city into surrender, had withdrawn his ships into the Gulf to get out of the range of the Confederate shore batteries.

Late that afternoon, the lookout aboard the *Brooklyn* spied a three-masted ship approaching from the open Gulf. The vessel stopped 12 miles offshore, arousing Commodore Bell's suspicions. Since the *Brooklyn* was immobilized by engine repairs, the *Hatteras*, an iron side-wheeler that had been built as an excursion boat, was sent to investigate the newcomer. The trim stranger moved away under topsails only, allowing the much slower *Hatteras* to draw closer. The captain of the *Hatteras*, Lieutenant Commander Homer C. Blake, sensed that he was being lured away from the fleet, but he could only pursue and prepare for an attack.

About 20 miles from the Federal squadron, the stranger lay to. By now night had fallen, but the vessel was still visible in the darkness. The *Hatteras* closed to within 100 yards. There Blake stopped and hailed the ship, demanding her identity.

"This is Her Britannic Majesty's steamer *Petrel*," came the reply. Reassured by this news, the *Hatteras* identified herself and asked for permission to send an inspection party to confirm the *Petrel's* registry, a belligerent's right under international law. Permission was granted.

Before the inspection boat had gone a length, a clear voice rang across the water, "This is the Confederate States steamer *Alabama*. Fire!"

Within 13 minutes the *Hatteras* was sinking. Except for two Yankees killed in the fight, the *Alabama* rescued all hands, including five wounded men, then she ran out of harm's way to Jamaica. The *Alabama*, under Captain Raphael Semmes, had deliberately picked a fight with a Union warship, albeit a weak one, and she had whipped the enemy with ease and aplomb. The *Alabama* and her crew now resumed their real mission—to destroy or capture Union merchantmen. Hers was a career of devastation with few equals in modern sea warfare.

The *Alabama* was the most feared and the most successful of the Confederate commerce raiders, but she had a fair amount of destructive company. At various times more than a dozen vessels joined in the work, though no more than five were in operation simultaneously. All were part of the design of Stephen R. Mallory, the Confederate Secretary of the Navy, to attack the Union in its vulnerable merchant fleet.

Semmes Motto "I am here"

The mustachioed scourge of Union merchant shipping, Captain Raphael Semmes flaunts a cutlass and the Jolly Roger in this caricature by Thomas Nast, the political satirist.

The best of the ships—the *Alabama, Florida* and *Shenandoah*—had been secured in England by Confederate Navy agent James Bulloch, and they had been carefully built or adapted for their missions. They were powered by steam engines, which gave them speed and maneuverability. But since steamships of the day were severely limited in range by their capacity for fuel, the raiders were equipped with full sets of sails.

These raiders were versatile in ways other than the sail-or-steam option. The guns that each carried made her a formidable fighting vessel, though she had to serve so many purposes that a comparable warship, designed only for fighting, was superior to her. For several reasons, the raider was a commodious vessel. She needed considerable space for her large ship's complement, which included the crew and sometimes a contingent of Confederate marines. She needed a large storage area, too, for confiscated Union cargoes. And she needed a great deal of space for a captured Union crew or crews, who had to be conveyed to the nearest port after their ship had been destroyed at sea or taken over by a Confederate prize crew.

Bulloch had provided excellent vessels. Mallory provided captains to match them. Like their ships, Raphael Semmes of the *Alabama*, John Newland Maffitt of the *Florida* and James Iredell Waddell of the *Shenandoah* were well suited to their missions. They had the strong professional background and broad experience that came with many years of service in the prewar U.S. Navy. They had the self-reliance, the planning ability and managerial skills, the steady judgment and sheer stamina needed for their long, lonely cruises. They had the tact and persuasiveness to act as diplomats in foreign ports.

And they were opportunists and improvisers of the first water.

Semmes had all of these command qualities in ample measure, but none of the characteristics that often went with them. He was not large or physically strong, and in manner he was not flamboyant, aggressive or demanding. He was a man who stayed much alone, avoiding camaraderie with his officers. He led quietly, fairly and firmly. Said his old colleague Captain James Bulloch, "If circumstance had ever placed him at the head of a fleet, I feel sure that he would have achieved important and notable results."

It was a reasonable surmise: All his life Raphael Semmes had made the most of circumstances. Orphaned as a young Maryland boy and raised by an uncle and aunt, he joined the Navy as a midshipman at the age of 16. After six years of study, mostly at sea but also in the Norfolk officers' training school, he graduated near the top of his class. Then, encouraged to take a leave of absence because there were too many officers for the peacetime Navy, Semmes began to study law, which he followed as a parallel career during later interludes of inactive duty. In the 1840s he established his permanent home in Mobile, Alabama, and became a dyed-in-the-cotton Southerner.

Semmes first came to public notice in 1844 when, as captain of the steamer U.S.S. *Poinsett*, he transported an American diplomat on a peace mission to Mexico and escorted him to Mexico City. The mission failed, and after the outbreak of war Semmes repeated his journey to Mexico City, this time accompanying the U.S. invasion army.

After the War, Semmes capitalized on his Mexican experiences by recounting them in a book that became highly popular. In turn

Leaving the captured Union clipper *Harvey Birch* in flames, boarding parties from the Confederate commerce raider *Nashville* row back to their ship, bringing with them the 31-man Yankee crew. The *Harvey Birch*, destroyed off the Irish coast on November 19, 1861, was the second-largest merchantman seized by raiders during the War.

this success helped him to develop his law practice in Mobile and to enter local politics.

All this ended abruptly in 1856 when Semmes was recalled to active duty. Two years later he was assigned to Washington as Secretary of the Lighthouse Board. Among the politicians he came to know there was a Senator from Mississippi, Jefferson Davis.

On February 15, 1861, even as the government of the Confederate States of America was being organized, Semmes resigned his U.S. commission and reported immediately to President Davis' Committee on Naval Affairs in Montgomery, Alabama. Davis sent him into the North to recruit trained mechanics and to purchase military and naval supplies. Semmes did his job well. The skilled workers and matériel he assembled were invaluable in developing an ordnance program for the infant Confederacy.

In April, Semmes returned to Montgomery, and on the 17th, just after the attack on Fort Sumter, he called on Navy Secretary Mallory to discuss commerce raiding in general. Mallory said that vessels available for the purpose were of disappointing quality, and he showed Semmes a descriptive report of one such ship. After studying the report, Semmes said, "Give me that ship. I think I can make her answer the purpose."

Semmes had chosen as the first Confederate Navy commerce raider the packet *Habana*, a steamer of 520 tons lying in New Orleans. She had been built for the trade between New Orleans and Havana and could carry only five days' worth of fuel for her low-pressure engines. She had no accommodations for a fighting crew.

This vessel, renamed the *Sumter*, was refurbished with a strengthened main deck, a berth deck, shell room, powder magazine and additional coal bunkers. Then she was armed with an 8-inch pivot gun and four 32-pound howitzers. Semmes and his Confederate officers assembled a crew of 92 sailors, including 20 marines. The crewmen were to receive pay nominally a little higher than either merchant sailors or Navy seamen, but actually much higher; they would be paid in gold rather than inflated Confederate paper money. But what attracted the men most was a share in any money made by selling captured ships or confiscated cargoes.

Semmes hoped to begin operations before the newly declared Union blockade could take effect. But his hopes were dashed when the U.S.S. *Brooklyn* and *Powhatan* appeared off the mouth of the Mississippi late in May. Those ships, soon joined by others, sealed off the passes at the mouth of the river.

The *Sumter* was finally ready for the sea on June 18. Semmes took her downriver to await an opportunity to run out. He was anchored at Head of Passes at the mouth of the river when on June 30 the *Brooklyn* left her station to chase a sail. Semmes hauled anchor and steamed down the Pass a Loutre and into the open Gulf beyond. The *Brooklyn* sighted the *Sumter*, came about and attempted to head her off. But Semmes changed course, forcing the *Brooklyn* to sail at an unfavorable angle to the wind. The Federal ship dropped gradually astern and the *Sumter* sailed away over the horizon.

Three days later, Semmes made his first capture off the coast of Cuba. The prey was a 700-ton bark named the *Golden Rocket*, out of Bangor, Maine. Neither the ownership nor the cargo of the *Golden Rocket* posed any foreign complications: She was a ship of U.S. registry traveling empty to pick up a cargo of Cuban sugar. By then Great Britain had de-clared itself neutral and other nations were following suit, which meant that most of the convenient Caribbean ports would not admit the *Golden Rocket* as a prize ship. This condition had immediately put a crimp on the privateers' business, and for all practical purposes it left Semmes no choice but to destroy the captive. He took aboard her master and crew, helped himself to her supplies and prepared to set the vessel on fire.

Crewmen ripped apart the straw-filled mattresses in the cabin and forecastle and slathered the kindling with butter and lard from the ship's stores. Once the fires were set, flames raced in every direction. Wrote Semmes: "The indraught into the burning ship's holds and cabins added every moment new fury to the flames, and now they could be heard roaring like the fires of a hundred furnaces in full blast. The forked tongues leaped into the rigging, newly tarred, ran rapidly up the shrouds. The intricate network of the cordage was traced, as with a pencil of fire, upon the black sky beyond, the many threads of flame twisting and writhing like so many serpents that had received their death wounds. The great main-mast tottered, reeled and fell over the ship's side into the sea, making a noise like that of the sturdy oak of the forest when it falls."

Semmes had no trouble locating more prey. The Union merchant fleet was composed largely of sailing ships, which rode the prevailing winds along well-known sea lanes. A commerce raider had merely to follow the sea lanes and she would come upon victims. Of course the Yankee merchantmen could leave the sea lanes and make a safer though slower voyage. But the shipowners were insured against loss, and they wanted swift trips to earn bigger profits. Captains who

The first Confederate Navy raider, the *Sumter*, looked like—and originally was—an undistinguished commercial steamer. But her captain, Raphael Semmes, wrote of her fondly: "Her lines were easy and graceful, and she had a sort of saucy air about her."

drifted for days without wind while their crews collected wages might well lose their commands and reputations.

As Semmes quickly learned, not only was it hard to profit by captured ships and confiscated cargoes, it was extremely difficult to sustain his own operations in the face of international law, and the regulations of neutrals. Like the more conventional warships of belligerents, the *Sumter* was subject to various restrictions on the length of time she could spend in neutral ports. The crew could not improve on the ship's fighting capabilities, but could only make repairs necessary for seaworthiness. Perforce Semmes and his

fellow raider captains became masters at hoodwinking port authorities and breaking or evading local laws.

For example, some ports would not admit prizes even to convey ashore captured crewmen and passengers. This put great pressure on everyone in a ship as small as the *Sumter*. In such cases, Semmes often transferred the burdensome people to willing neutral ships or to Union merchantmen carrying a cargo belonging to a neutral. He and the Yankee captain would negotiate the release of the ship on what was called a ransom bond—a price based primarily on the value of that cargo. The Yankee captains signed papers calling for a bond to be paid to the Confederacy six months after a peace treaty was signed between the North and the South. (Of course, no Confederate government then existed to receive the bond.)

The raiders' depredations caused insurance rates to increase manifold. The same Yankee shipowners who had been indifferent to risking their insured ships and cargoes were no longer so casual about paying exorbitant insurance rates that minimized profits. To regain the low rates they transferred their ships to neutral registry, quickly eroding the huge U.S. merchant fleet. By the War's end more than 100 American ships had been switched to neutral flags.

Semmes took the *Sumter* through the Caribbean and along the South American coast for two months, then into the Atlantic. He made no effort to conceal his activities or to evade U.S. warships, few of which could then be spared from blockade duty.

Late in November of 1861, Semmes narrowly escaped a Federal warship and set sail for Spain. The *Sumter* reached Gibraltar on January 19, 1862, arriving without coal and in bad repair after a rough passage. There Semmes met with enemy opposition of a sort that would haunt him throughout his wartime career. The U.S. consul at Gibraltar, Horatio J. Sprague, used his influence to prevent private dealers from selling coal to the *Sumter*. Semmes also tried in vain to buy coal from the British authorities. In the meantime the U.S.S. *Tuscarora*, and later the *Ino* and the *Kearsarge*, arrived on the scene and blockaded the *Sumter*.

Semmes resigned himself to the futility of his position. With the permission of Confederate commissioner James M. Mason in London, he discharged his crew and left a dozen men behind as caretakers of the disabled vessel. Semmes and most of his officers departed for London, intending to return to their beleaguered homeland. But Semmes would meet the *Kearsarge* again.

During her six-month career as a commerce raider, the *Sumter* had captured 18 ships. Semmes relinquished two after their captains pledged ransom bonds. Two merchantmen were recaptured by the Union after Semmes sent aboard his own prize crews; one prize was retaken when the Yankee captives overcame Semmes's prize crew and the other when she failed to run the blockade at New Orleans. Semmes burned seven ships, and the Cuban authorities confiscated another seven to return to their Yankee owners. As for the trapped *Sumter*, a Confeder-

Distraught passengers aboard a Union merchant ship cluster around the worried captain as he watches Raphael Semmes's *Alabama* steam toward him in this 1863 engraving by Winslow Homer. Captain Semmes was amused by the alarm he inspired. "If that old buccaneer Blue Beard himself had appeared," he wrote, "the consternation could not have been greater."

ate officer offered her for sale. She was purchased at auction by a Liverpool merchant in December of 1862. She served briefly as a blockade-runner, then foundered off the coast of Normandy.

Semmes, homeward bound from England, was intercepted in Nassau and ordered back to England to take command of a ship that Captain Bulloch had contracted to build. The vessel was now nearing completion at Laird's shipyards in Birkenhead.

On his arrival in Liverpool, Semmes was recognized easily and often. He had quickly become a figure in the international press and, as his released captives had reported, he now sported a mustache noteworthy even in a period of outlandish hirsute adornments. It was a luxuriant handlebar, curving up and far outward to waxed points. It had inspired crewmen to nickname Semmes Old Beeswax, and it supplied him with a touch of the flamboyance he had hitherto lacked.

No doubt because he was conspicuous, Semmes took care not to violate the British Foreign Enlistment Act, which forbade recruiting or enlisting British subjects for service with foreign belligerents. Semmes did spend most of his time recruiting officers for his new ship, but he confined his efforts to the Confederate Navy officers from the *Sumter*. The most important of those to rejoin Semmes was First Lieutenant John McIntosh Kell, who became his executive officer. Through Bulloch, Semmes also managed to enlist a capable British surgeon, David Herbert Llewellyn.

Captain Bulloch had chartered the steamer *Bahama* to carry Semmes and his officers to the rendezvous with the *Enrica*, as the new construction was named, and the *Agrip-pina*, which would transport the future Confederate's ordnance, ammunition, stores and coal. The rendezvous of the three ships was completed on the 20th of August with the *Bahama's* arrival at the port of Praia da Vitória on Terceira in the Azores.

The conversion of the *Enrica* to a commerce raider was completed at the bay at Angra do Heroísmo. Semmes left his anchorage on August 24, 1862, and sailing a few miles off the coast to be outside neutral waters, he commissioned his ship the *Alabama*. He formally signed on a highly miscellaneous crew of about 85 seamen, who had been recruited by Captain Bulloch and half of whom had sailed the ship from England.

The new raider was 220 feet long, 32 feet abeam and barkentine rigged. Under steam alone she could make 10 knots, and under sail and steam combined she could reach a top speed of 13 knots. The ship's armament consisted of eight guns: one large Blakely 110-pounder rifled gun on a pivot forward, one 8-inch smoothbore gun amidships and six 32-pounders in broadside.

After commissioning the *Alabama*, Captain Semmes decided to attack the American whaling fleet in the Azores, a favorite feeding ground for whales from spring through September. On September 5, the lookout on the *Alabama* sighted the raider's first victim, the whaler *Ocmulgee* out of Edgartown, Massachusetts. Semmes followed the generally accepted practice of approaching a strange ship in disguise. He ran up a British flag, and after the whaler raised the U.S. flag, the *Alabama* struck its false colors and raised the Confederate ensign. The *Ocmulgee* had a dead whale lashed to her side and could not move. A party of Confederates was sent aboard the whaler. They removed the cap-

The C.S.S. "Florida" versus Union Shipping

CAPTAIN JOHN NEWLAND MAFFITT

"My instructions were brief and to the point, leaving much to the discretion but more to the torch," wrote John Newland Maffitt, the first captain of the Confederate Navy commerce raider *Florida*. He boldly sought out and burned Union merchantmen in Northern waters, venturing within 50 miles of New York Harbor and exciting hysteria ashore. Maffitt further confounded the U.S. Navy by outfitting a few prizes as miniature cruisers to extend his own destructive forays. One of these ships, the *Tacony*, captured 15 vessels in just two weeks.

The *Florida* herself took 23 prizes during Maffitt's seven-month cruise. And after he was relieved to recuperate from yellow fever, his successor, Captain Charles Morris, seized another 13 ships. All told, the *Florida* and the raiders she spawned captured more than four million dollars' worth of shipping—a total second only to that of the *Alabama*.

The *Florida's* career ended off Bahia, Brazil. Captain Morris anchored there on the night of October 4, 1864, unaware that the Federal steam sloop *Wachusett* was moored ahead of her in the harbor. Relying on peaceable assurances from the local U.S. consul, Morris began refitting his ship and gave half the crew shore leave. Three days later, the consul prevailed on Commander Napoleon Collins of the *Wachusett* to flout international law and ram the *Florida*. A glancing blow failed to sink her, so Collins' men boarded the raider and seized her crew; the prize was sailed to Hampton Roads. The lawless ambush infuriated Brazil and the European powers, forcing the United States to apologize. But before diplomats could arrange the *Florida's* return to Brazil, she collided with a U.S. Army transport and sank—an embarrassment to the U.S. Navy even in death.

A Confederate boarding party rows back to the *Florida* after setting fire to the *Jacob Bell*. The Yankee clipper carried merchandise worth two million dollars—the richest cargo captured by Confederate raiders.

The *Florida* (*center*) takes on coal and provisions off Funchal, Madeira, in February 1864. The U.S.S. *St. Louis* (*right background*) rides at anchor, waiting for the Confederate to leave the neutral harbor. But the Federal sailing sloop, lacking wind for pursuit, was unable to follow when the raider steamed away.

Slipping stealthily through a pitch black Brazilian harbor, the Federal sloop *Wachusett* rams the *Florida*, crushing her starboard bulwarks and snapping her mizzenmast like a matchstick.

tain and his 36 men, and later cast them adrift in their own whaleboats within easy reach of the Azores island of Flores. They took the Yankee's provisions, and set the ship on fire the next morning.

In two weeks of work in the Azores, Semmes captured and destroyed eight Yankee whalers, one schooner and one supply ship. The distressed seamen and passengers from each of the *Alabama's* victims were collected by the local U.S. consul, who hurried them home in a chartered ship. Upon their arrival in the United States, they and the stories they told invariably made lurid headlines in Northern newspapers. Semmes was called a pirate and accused—falsely—of torturing his prisoners.

After decimating the Union whaling fleet in the Azores, Semmes headed for the waters off Newfoundland and New England. He ravaged Yankee shipping there, destroying eight vessels and releasing three on ransom bond in 26 days of October. One of the ships he captured, the *Tonawanda*, had 30 women and children aboard. Wrote Semmes: "It was not possible to convert the *Alabama* into a nursery and set the stewards to serving pap to the babies. Although I made it a rule never to bond a ship if I could burn her, I released the *Tonawanda* on bond."

From the northern coast, Semmes headed south, bypassing Bermuda to the east. In December he haunted the Caribbean trade routes followed by the merchantmen, then made the side trip into the Gulf that brought him to Galveston in January of 1863.

The year 1863 was the heyday of the commerce cruisers. At least three of them— the *Alabama*, the *Georgia* and the *Florida*— were at sea at all times; among them they captured 67 Federal vessels, burning 51 and

releasing or bonding the rest. And these three were reinforced from time to time by prize ships that had been converted into raiders or tenders.

For many months, Lincoln and his naval strategists had been under heavy pressure from Northern shipowners to mount a killer campaign against the Confederate cruisers. They had refused to comply at the expense of weakening the blockade. But as the U.S. Navy grew from 427 vessels in December of 1862 to 588 a year later, warships could occasionally be spared for duties other than maintaining the blockade. A few warships were stationed in or near the ports most likely to be visited by the Confederate cruisers, and a few patrolled the busy trade lanes in hopes that a raider would show up. Semmes and other captains knew that the enemy was growing more numerous and more dangerous. But the hunting was too good for them to realize that their time was running out.

Semmes had started the year auspiciously with the sinking of the U.S.S. *Hatteras* and the capture of 13 other ships by the end of March. In April, the *Alabama* left the Gulf and appeared off Brazil, a crossroads of international trade routes. Semmes worked the coast of South America for three months and captured 15 ships. Then, prudently deciding to move on before the U.S. Navy descended upon him, he sailed for the African coast.

The *Alabama* arrived at Saldanha Bay, 60 miles northeast of Cape Town, on July 29. After cruising the coast for a while, Semmes headed for the open port of Cape Town for repairs and provisioning. Word of his approach had preceded him, carried by neutral ships, and many townspeople gathered on hilltop vantage points to watch the famous raider's arrival. They saw much more than

At anchor off Cape Town, Captain Raphael Semmes (*foreground*) and First Lieutenant John McIntosh Kell, his executive officer, lounge by the *Alabama's* pivot-mounted 8-inch smoothbore Dahlgren gun.

they expected. As the *Alabama* reached a point about five miles outside the entrance to Table Bay, she chanced upon the Yankee bark *Sea Bride*.

Wrote the editor of the *Cape Argus:* "The *Alabama* fired a gun and brought her to. Like a cat watching and playing with a victimised mouse, Captain Semmes permitted the prize to draw off a few yards, and he then pounced upon her. The *Alabama* first sailed round the Yankee from stem to stern, and stern to stem again. The way that fine, saucy, rakish craft was handled was worth riding a hundred miles to see. She went around the bark like a toy, making a complete circle, and leaving an even margin of water between herself and her prize of not more than 20 yards. This done, she sent a boat with the prize crew off, took possession in the name of the Confederate States and sent the bark to sea. The *Alabama* then made for port."

Semmes disposed of the *Sea Bride* in a way that stretched but did not quite break international law. He had the prize sailed up the west coast of Africa to the land of the Hottentots, where he felt it was possible to do business without entanglements. There he sold the *Sea Bride* to a less-than-scrupulous buyer from Cape Town who, realizing that Semmes could not deliver a clear title to the ship, paid him only one third of her market value, $16,940 in cash.

For about six weeks the *Alabama* operated out of Cape Town without making another capture. But no one minded. When in port, the captain and his officers were invited to dinner and interviewed by the press. And after many months at sea the sailors made

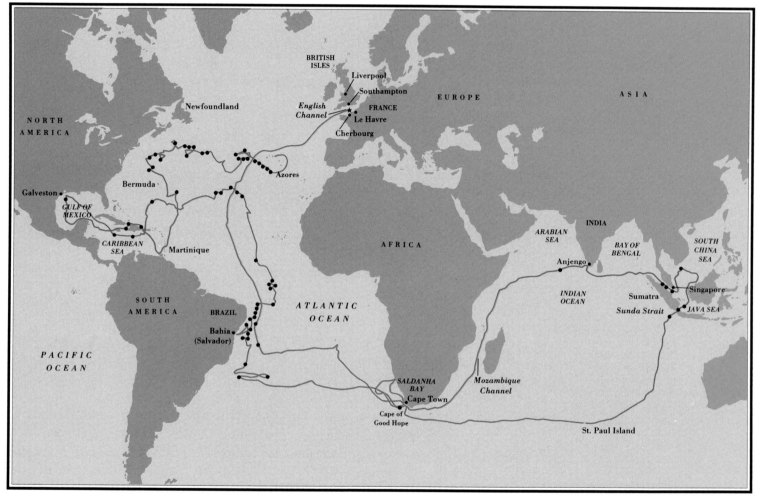

the most of their safe harbor. Too much, in fact: Some of the men were reported drunk and disorderly.

Semmes was not at all surprised; the crew had caused just such disturbances in Martinique and Jamaica. Actually, except for the officers, the ship's complement was never more than an unreliable polyglot collection. In spite of Semmes's continuing drills, the crew was simply too unstable to be forged into a smooth-working team. Sailors kept jumping ship, and replacements were continually being recruited at ports of call and from the crews of captured ships. In exas-

peration, Semmes wrote that August: "I have a precious set of rascals on board, faithless in the matter of abiding by their contracts, liars, thieves and drunkards."

Tired of the poor hunting around Cape Town, the *Alabama* set course for the Far East. Semmes took his ship across the Indian Ocean, through the Sunda Strait, into the Java and China Seas. He had captured and burned six Yankee ships in the Orient by the end of 1863, bringing his year's total to 36. On pulling into Singapore, he found 22 American ships in port and claimed to have frightened them ashore. "The birds had all

The destructive cruise of the C.S.S. *Alabama* covered 75,000 miles, her outbound journey *(green)* commencing in the Azores and her return trip *(red)* ending at Cherbourg 22 months later. Of the 65 Union merchantmen she captured *(black dots)*, the 52 that were burned had been appraised at $4,613,914—nearly 20 times the *Alabama's* own cost.

taken to cover," Semmes wrote, "and there was no such thing as flushing them." Disappointed, he turned the *Alabama* westward, sailing to the southern tip of India and then through the Mozambique Channel back to the Cape of Good Hope. Along the way he destroyed only one Yankee vessel.

The *Alabama* was beginning to show the wear and tear of almost 20 months at sea. "Her boilers were burned out," wrote Lieutenant Kell, "and her machinery was sadly in want of repairs. She was loose in every joint, her seams were open, and the copper on her bottom was in rolls." Semmes decided to head for England or France for a thorough overhaul of his ship.

As the *Alabama* beat north along the Atlantic coast of Africa, Semmes captured two Yankee ships, took their crews and passengers aboard, then put the vessels to the torch. But he had lost his zest for the campaign. He reflected despondently on reports of Union victories in newspapers he had acquired in Cape Town. He wrote: "Might it not be that, after all our trials and sacrifices, the cause for which we were struggling would be lost? The thought was hard to bear."

On June 10, 1864, the *Alabama* reached the Cape of the Hague on the Normandy coast, picked up a French pilot and dropped anchor in the port of Cherbourg. Semmes immediately requested permission to land his prisoners and put the *Alabama* into dry dock. The next day he took to his bunk with a cold and fever. The French authorities refused his request for dock space, explaining—as Semmes knew—that the only docks in Cherbourg belonged to the government and were reserved for the French Navy; permission to use them could be granted only by the Emperor Napoleon III, who was away from Paris on a vacation. The authorities recommended that Semmes move the *Alabama* to Le Havre or another port with private facilities.

But Semmes was confident that permission eventually would be granted. After all, the French government had been a strong supporter of the Confederacy, which in turn supported Napoleon III's venture in Mexico. Semmes put his 38 prisoners ashore and gave his men the run of the town.

News of the *Alabama*'s arrival in Cherbourg swept across Europe. Soon the hotels in Cherbourg were filled with fashionable visitors eager to see the famous Confederate cruiser and talk with her celebrated crew.

On June 12, the day after the *Alabama* docked in Cherbourg, the American Minister in Paris telegraphed news of her arrival to the U.S.S. *Kearsarge*, riding at anchor 300 miles away, off the Dutch coast near Flushing. The commander of the *Kearsarge*, Captain John A. Winslow, was urged to hurry to Cherbourg before the *Alabama* could escape.

Winslow, who had been a shipmate of Semmes's during the Mexican War, knew his adversary and did not need the Minister's advice to hurry. He fired a gun to recall his crew and quickly put the *Kearsarge* under way. Winslow was determined that Semmes would not elude him again, as he had in the *Sumter* at Gibraltar.

The *Alabama* and the *Kearsarge* had almost equal dimensions, but their capabilities were considerably different. The Federal ship's best guns, two 11-inch Dahlgrens mounted on pivots along the center line, were far superior at close quarters to the 110-pounder Blakely and the 8-inch smoothbore on which Semmes chiefly depended; and her

Armed with spyglasses, festive Frenchmen hasten from Sunday Mass to Cherbourg's seaside bluffs to witness the duel between the U.S.S. *Kearsarge* and the C.S.S. *Alabama,* discernible as smoky smudges about six miles offshore. A crowd estimated at 15,000 watched the battle.

broadside threw 365 pounds of metal, about one third more than the *Alabama's.* The *Kearsarge* had a superbly drilled American crew of 163. The Confederate had 149 mixed mercenaries of uneven training. The Yankee was two months out of dry dock, her engines in excellent working order.

The captains were evenly matched. Winslow, a North Carolinian, was two years younger than Semmes, but like Semmes he had some 35 years of Navy experience. Although Winslow's record was known only within the U.S. Navy, he was a skillful captain. Only in appearance was he outshone by the trim Confederate captain. Winslow was paunchy, balding, going blind in one eye. In facial adornment his scraggly ruff of graying whiskers was hardly worth comparing with Semmes's magnificent handlebar.

Winslow arrived at Cherbourg on June 14. As the *Kearsarge* approached the port, Wins-

low spotted the Confederate ship; he circled about and anchored off the breakwater. The two crews studied each other's ship with an intensity known only to men who expected to fight broadside to broadside.

Immediately upon sighting the *Kearsarge,* Semmes ordered 100 tons of coal delivered to his ship and started his crew on the work of preparing the *Alabama* for battle. He summoned Lieutenant Kell to his cabin and said, "I am going out to fight the *Kearsarge;* what do you think of it?"

They candidly discussed their disadvantages in a fight. In addition to their lighter broadside, they had unreliable ammunition; their powder, fuses and caps had become defective during the many months at sea. To their alarm, one out of every three shells had failed to explode.

Nevertheless, Semmes in pure bravado sent a note asking the Confederate agent in

Cherbourg to challenge the Yankee warship. The message said: "I desire you to say to the U.S. consul that my intention is to fight the *Kearsarge* as soon as I can make the necessary arrangements. I beg she will not depart before I am ready to go out." When Captain Winslow and his officers received Semmes's challenge, they suspected a trick and prepared for it.

Work on the *Alabama* proceeded steadily. Nonessential spars and rigging were removed and the deck was holystoned. Small arms, guns and swords were cleaned. The brasswork was polished to a high gleam. The ship's boilers were repaired and the crew was run through gun drills.

On Saturday afternoon Semmes sent the Confederate agent his ship's valuables: a collection of chronometers taken from his victims; the ship's funds, including 4,700 gold sovereigns; and the ransom bonds of the 10 ships that he had released. He informed the French authorities that he would be fighting the next day, then attended Mass. Returning to the ship early in the evening, Semmes went straight to bed. So did his officers and crew, despite many invitations from admirers on shore.

Sunday was a perfect day for the fight. It was bright, clear and cool, with a breeze just strong enough to clear away the smoke of the battle. A crowd in the thousands gathered on Cherbourg's roofs and heights in sight of the English Channel. Fanfare in the newspapers had fetched trainloads of Parisians to watch the contest and enjoy the festive occasion. Some spectators carried tiny Confederate flags to wave for their heroes.

At 9:45 a.m., the *Alabama* hoisted anchor and set out toward the Channel. She was escorted by a French ironclad frigate, the *Couronne,* sent to make certain that the combatants met outside the three-mile limit. In their wake followed a flotilla of spectator craft. The *Alabama's* passage through the harbor and out the West Pass to the Channel was accompanied by hearty cheers from the crowd and a ship that carried a band playing "Dixie."

As the *Alabama* rounded the breakwater protecting the entrance to the port, Semmes saw the *Kearsarge* about seven miles to the northeast. The Federal ship turned and bore off northeastward as if trying to avoid the engagement. But Semmes knew better. To him the move meant that the *Kearsarge* was intent on steaming well beyond the three-mile limit so that the two ships might fight to the finish, with neither being able to reach the protection of neutral waters.

Captain Winslow was reading the Sunday service to his crew when the alarm came from the lookout. He closed his prayer book and ordered the beat to quarters.

At that moment, Semmes was delivering a romantic speech to inspire his assembled crew. "Officers and seamen of the *Alabama!*" he shouted from an uncomfortable perch on top of a gun carriage. "The name of your ship has become a household word wherever civilization extends! Shall that name be tarnished by defeat? The thing is impossible! Remember that the eyes of all Europe are at this moment upon you. The flag that floats over you is that of a young republic which bids defiance to her enemies whenever and wherever found! Show the world that you know how to uphold it! Go to your quarters!"

Semmes then assumed his battle station on the quarterdeck near the mizzenmast. From this elevated position he would be able to witness the action throughout the battle.

In the meantime, the *Kearsarge* had turned about and begun closing with the *Alabama.* When the two vessels were about a mile apart, Semmes opened fire.

Winslow held his fire for several minutes more. Finally, at a range of about half a mile, he commenced firing with his starboard battery. Semmes had to veer strongly to port to keep his stern from being raked, but this allowed the *Kearsarge* to close the range. As the *Alabama* turned back to starboard, her enemy followed suit. The two warships began to travel in parallel circles. They steamed clockwise, drifting westward with the current, confronting each other at a slowly diminishing range as the *Kearsarge,* the swifter of the pair, was able to tighten each succeeding circle. All the while, the two vessels traded broadsides.

The *Alabama* drew first blood, knocking out three Union sailors manning the after Dahlgren. But otherwise her shells were having little effect upon the *Kearsarge.* One shell from the Blakely hit the enemy's sternpost but proved to be a dud. Other hits did little more damage, even after Semmes switched from explosive shells to solid shot.

Meanwhile the 11-inch shells from the *Kearsarge's* Dahlgrens were wreaking havoc on the *Alabama.* Three shells in a row entered through the 8-inch pivot gunport. The first swept away the forward men of the gun crew; the second killed one man and wounded several others; the third struck the breast of the gun carriage and spun it around on the deck. The decks of the *Alabama* were littered with dead and wounded men.

The ships fought their way through six full circles. As the seventh commenced, Semmes was slightly wounded in the right hand; he had it bound and a sling rigged by a quartermaster. His ship was heavily damaged and listing to starboard from hits along the water line. Fearing that the *Alabama* would go down, Semmes ordered Kell to make all possible sail and head for the coast.

The ship reversed direction to reach the shore. Kell was proud of the crew's smart execution of the maneuver. But the *Alabama* in fact was done. The quarterdeck was so cluttered with mangled bodies that Kell had to have them thrown overboard in order to transfer men from starboard to fight the port guns now facing the *Kearsarge.* The engineer reported that the boiler fires were out, and Kell went below to see how long the ship could float. There he found, as he wrote, that Surgeon Llewellyn was "poised to work, but the table and the patient upon it had been swept away by an 11-inch shell, which opened in the side of the ship an aperture that was fast filling the ship with water."

Kell returned immediately and informed Semmes that the *Alabama* could not last 10 minutes. "Then, sir," responded Semmes, "cease firing, shorten sail and haul down the colors; it will never do in this 19th Century for us to go down, and the decks covered with our gallant wounded."

From 500 yards across the water, Winslow watched the Confederate ensign being lowered. But he suspected a trick and ordered another broadside with every gun that could be brought to bear. He did not order a cease-fire until a white flag was run up the stern of the *Alabama.*

Soon a dinghy from the *Alabama* approached, filled with wounded men. Someone shouted for the Yankees to send boats to rescue the survivors.

The *Alabama's* guns had damaged or de-

CAPTAIN JAMES IREDELL WADDELL

The "Shenandoah's" Fiery Journey

In October 1864, the Confederacy's indefatigable agents sent the merchant steamer *Sea King* from London to a rendezvous near the island of Madeira, 400 miles off the coast of North Africa. There they armed the swift 230-foot vessel with eight guns and renamed her the *Shenandoah*. She was commanded by a 40-year-old former U.S. Navy lieutenant named James Iredell Waddell, a stubborn North Carolinian and a consummate seaman.

Waddell's orders represented a shrewd change in raiding tactics. Rather than roving the North Atlantic, now teeming with hostile warships, he was to ravage the 58-ship Yankee whaling fleet in the North Pacific. After seizing nearly a dozen merchantmen en route through the South Atlantic, Waddell opened the whaling campaign in the West Pacific, taking four ships on April 1, 1865. Two months later he reached the icy Sea of Okhotsk off the Siberian coast; he found only one whaler, but her reprobate second mate volunteered to pilot him to the elusive fleet.

Guided by this turncoat, the *Shenandoah* entered the Bering Sea on June 16 and in one week seized six prizes, burning five and bonding one to carry the dispossessed Yankee sailors. The last of these ships carried newspapers dated April 14, which reported General Robert E. Lee's surrender and also Confederate vows of continued resistance.

Refusing to believe the War was lost, Waddell pursued his campaign. In five days he captured 18 more whalers and burned all but three. When ice forced him to leave the whaling grounds, Waddell headed for San Francisco; he harbored a wild scheme to hold the city hostage under his guns. On the way, he overtook a British bark and learned that the War was indeed over. The *Shenandoah's* total of prizes stood at 38.

Rather than surrender to Union authorities, who he thought might hang him for piracy, Waddell sailed 17,000 miles to Liverpool. He surrendered to the British on November 6, 1865—seven months after the War ended.

Dodging ice floes, the *Shenandoah* steams away from the nine whalers she set afire in June 1865. The vessels had gathered around a foundering whaler, allowing the *Shenandoah* to capture the entire flotilla.

After sailing 58,000 miles on a 13-month odyssey, the *Shenandoah* struck this last Confederate ensign of the War in Liverpool harbor.

stroyed all save two of the *Kearsarge's* boats. Winslow sent them, and later the unloaded Confederate dinghy, to pick up the survivors, who were thrashing about in the water. But it was clear to the Yankees that the three boats would not be enough for the rescue. An English steam yacht named the *Deerhound* drew closer, and Captain Winslow shouted to her through his speaking trumpet, "For God's sake, do what you can to save them!"

Semmes and Kell were among the last to abandon the sinking *Alabama*. Kell stripped to his shirt and underwear and plunged into the Channel. Semmes kept his trousers, his waistcoat and his dignity. He cast his sword into the water and then followed it himself.

The *Alabama* sank at 12:24 p.m., 90 minutes after firing her first shot. The ship's last moments were agony to Semmes and Kell as they struggled to keep themselves afloat in the water. Semmes later wrote, "We had buried her at sea as we had christened her, and she was safe from the polluting touch of the hated Yankee!"

A boat from the *Deerhound* picked up the Confederate officers. Semmes was immediately recognized and hidden under a tarpaulin. When a boat from the *Kearsarge* came alongside and a Federal seaman asked for Semmes, Kell replied, "He's drowned."

The *Deerhound* began to pull away from the scene. The owner said to Semmes, "I think every man has been picked up. Where shall I land you?" Semmes replied, "I am now under the English colors, and the sooner you put me with my officers and men on English soil, the better."

The sea battle was over. The *Kearsarge* had suffered three wounded, one of whom later died. The *Alabama* had 43 casualties, about half of them killed or drowned.

Winslow put in at Cherbourg, paroled his prisoners and proceeded to Paris, where he received a victor's welcome. In the United States, he was acclaimed by the press and a grateful nation. On President Lincoln's recommendation, Congress gave Winslow a vote of thanks and a promotion to commodore dating from the day of his victory, June 19. In turn, Winslow sent Lincoln a section of the *Kearsarge's* sternpost, with the 110-pound dud still embedded in it.

Semmes and Kell were landed at Southampton by the *Deerhound*. There Semmes paid off his crew and sent allotments to the kin of the dead. He received a sword from sundry admirers, including officers of the Royal Navy, to replace the one he had thrown into the Channel.

After a roundabout trip, Semmes returned to the South, was promoted to rear admiral, and assumed command of eight ironclads and gunboats on the James River during the final convulsions of the Confederate armies in Virginia. As Union forces closed in on Semmes's squadron, the raider captain who had burned 59 Union ships at sea ended up burning his own small fleet to prevent it from falling into Federal hands. Semmes finally surrendered at Greensboro, North Carolina, on May 1, 1865.

Semmes was later arrested and indicted for piracy. After spending four months in prison, he was released and reinstated on parole by President Andrew Johnson. He returned to Mobile in 1868 and lived out his days practicing law and writing about his exploits aboard the *Alabama*.

The demise of the *Alabama* signaled the beginning of the end for the commerce raiders. Captain John Maffitt's *Florida* continued operations with diminishing success until October of 1864, when a U.S. steam sloop forced her to surrender in the neutral Brazilian port of Bahia. The *Florida* was quickly replaced by the C.S.S. *Shenandoah,* bought in England by agent Bulloch and assigned to Captain James Waddell. But the *Shenandoah* waged her campaign in the remote North Pacific after the War had ended, and she was never more than the quixotic champion of a lost cause.

Altogether, the commerce raiders—the principal offensive weapon of the Confederate Navy—destroyed 257 Yankee vessels, or about 5 per cent of the Union merchant fleet. And yet that remarkable performance had no measurable effect on the blockade or on the Union's maritime trade. The raiders' main contributions were to bolster Confederate morale—and to enlarge the annals of sea adventure.

As an offensive weapon, the blockade was much more effective than the commerce raiders. Exactly how effective was quite another matter.

Until just a few months before the War's end, blockade-runners continued to scurry in and out of Southern ports, evading and outwitting the Union squadrons. Even as late as 1864, two out of every three blockade-running attempts along the entire Confederate coast were successful. And one port alone—Wilmington, North Carolina—exported about $65 million worth of cotton in the year before its fall to a Union assault early in 1865.

In exchange for Southern cotton, the Confederacy received from blockade-runners a continuous if inadequate supply of rifles, artillery pieces and munitions, to say nothing of perfume, satins and corset stays. All told, about 8,500 successful trips were made through the Federal blockade, whereas approximately 1,500 blockade-running vessels were captured or destroyed. Obviously the United States Navy never came close to its objective of making the blockade 100 per cent effective, and up to the closing months of the War a runner stood at least a 50-50 chance of slipping through the Union cordon.

For all that, the impact of the blockade on the course of the War was enormous. It greatly constricted the South's commerce, permitting her to export only small quantities of cotton and forcing her to buy supplies dear. This drained the Confederacy of its limited supplies of specie, inaugurating spectacular inflation at home and undermining its credit overseas. And once the Confederacy acted to lift its voluntary and ill-advised embargo of cotton, it discovered that the blockade severely limited exports of this precious commodity. In dramatic contrast to the 10 million bales that were shipped in the last three antebellum years, only one million bales were shipped in the last three years of the War. All told, the Federal blockade reduced the South's foreign trade by more than two thirds, just at the time when a vast increase in this exchange was needed to carry on the war effort.

In short, it was succor only, not sustenance, that filtered through the blockade to the beleaguered Confederacy. And even though the War was decided on the battlefield, not on the blockade line, it surely would have been a different war had the United States Navy not stood silent guard along the Southern coasts.

Swan Song for a Commerce Raider

'Here she comes! The *Alabama!*'' cried a lookout aboard the U.S.S. *Kearsarge* on the 19th of June, 1864. ''She's heading straight for us!'' shouted a Federal officer.

At last, after five days of waiting outside the French port of Cherbourg, Captain John A. Winslow and his crew saw the formidable commerce raider C.S.S. *Alabama*—commanded by the legendary Captain Raphael Semmes—emerging to fight them to the death. ''It made our hair stick right up straight,'' said a Marine corporal.

At a range of 900 yards, the two ships began moving in circles, firing broadside after broadside. It soon became apparent that the *Kearsarge* had the edge on her enemy in speed and armament. Besides, the Confederate gunners were firing so rapidly that few of their shots hit the *Kearsarge*,

Captain John A. Winslow (*third from left*) and other officers of the U.S.S. *Kearsarge* gather on her main deck before their fight with the C.S.S. *Alabama*.

while the Federal gunners were firing slowly and accurately—and cheering wildly whenever a shot found its mark.

Captain Winslow had told his crew three days earlier: "I will give you one hour to take the *Alabama*, and I think you can do it!" It now seemed that the men of the *Kearsarge* would prove their captain right.

The course of the running battle between the *Kearsarge* and the *Alabama* on June 19, 1864, is traced on a Union map of the English Channel. Beginning in the northeast *(upper right)*, the *Kearsarge* pursued the Confederate vessel through seven full circles; all the while, each ship tried to bring her broadside to bear on her opponent's vulnerable stern.

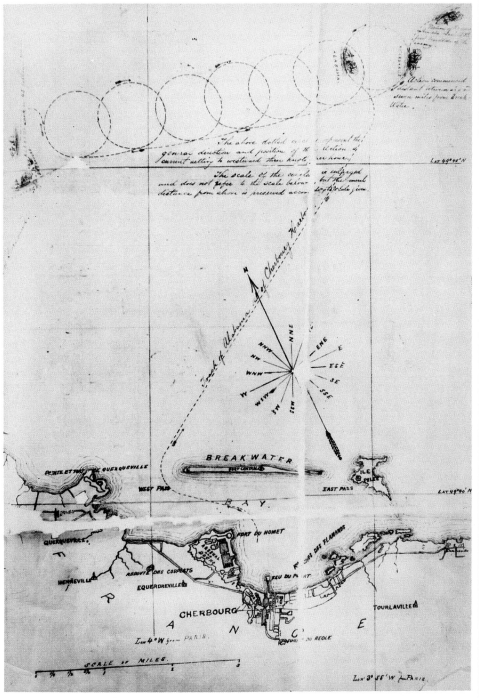

> "All the divisions! Aim low for the water line! Fire!
> Load and fire as rapidly as possible!"

CAPTAIN JOHN A. WINSLOW, U.S.S. *KEARSARGE*

Chasing the *Alabama* in a circle off Cherbourg, France, the *Kearsarge (foreground)* exchanges heavy broadsides with the Confederate Navy raider. The two ships,

An exploding shell from the Kearsarge's powerful 11-inch cannon wreaks havoc aboard the Alabama. The Confederate executive officer reported that one such shell, ripping through one of his ship's gunports, wiped out half a gun crew like a sponge erasing a blackboard.

Aboard the *Kearsarge*, crewmen of an 11-inch gun watch fascinated as the stricken *Alabama* lowers her flag in defeat. Captain Winslow, looking on at far left, praised his men for their "coolness and fortitude" under fire.

"*Nothing could restrain the enthusiasm of our men. Cheer succeeded cheer; caps were thrown in the air or overboard; jackets were discarded; sanguine of victory, the men were shouting as each projectile took effect.*"

SURGEON JOHN M. BROWNE, U.S.S. *KEARSARGE*

> "*As the gallant vessel, the most beautiful I ever beheld, plunged down to her grave,*
> *I had it on my tongue to call to the men who were struggling in the water to give three*
> *cheers for her, but the dead that were floating around me and the deep sadness*
> *I felt at parting with the noble ship that had been my home so long deterred me.*"
>
> EXECUTIVE OFFICER JOHN McINTOSH KELL, C.S.S. *ALABAMA*

BIBLIOGRAPHY

Books

Adams, Ephraim Douglass, *Great Britain and the American Civil War*. Russell & Russell, 1924.

Albion, Robert Greenhalgh, and Jennie Barnes Pope, *Sea Lanes in Wartime: The American Experience, 1775-1945*. Archon Books, 1968.

Anderson, Bern, *By Sea and by River*. Alfred A. Knopf, 1962.

Anderson, Edward C., *Confederate Foreign Agent: The European Diary of Major Edward C. Anderson*. Confederate Publishing Company, 1976.

Bailey, Thomas A.:
America Faces Russia: Russian-American Relations from Early Times to Our Day. Peter Smith, 1964.
A Diplomatic History of the American People. Appleton-Century Crofts, 1958.

Baxter, James Phinney, III, *The Introduction of the Ironclad Warship*. Harvard University Press, 1933.

Beam, Philip C., *Winslow Homer's Magazine Engravings*. Harper & Row, 1979.

Bennett, Frank M., *The Steam Navy of the United States*. Greenwood Press, Publishers, 1974.

Besse, S. B., *C.S. Ironclad Virginia*. The Mariners' Museum, Museum Publication No. 4, 1937.

Boatner, Mark Mayo, III, *The Civil War Dictionary*. David McKay Company, Inc., 1959.

Boykin, Edward, *Sea Devil of the Confederacy: The Story of the Florida and Her Captain, John Newland Maffitt*. Funk & Wagnalls Company, 1959.

Boynton, Charles B., *The History of the Navy during the Rebellion*. D. Appleton and Company, 1868.

Bradlee, Francis B. C., *Blockade Running during the Civil War: And the Effect of Land and Water Transportation on the Confederacy*. Porcupine Press, 1974.

Bradlow, Edna and Frank, *Here Comes the Alabama: The Career of a Confederate Raider*. A. A. Balkema, Cape Town, 1958.

Bulloch, James D., *The Secret Service of the Confederate States in Europe*, Vol. 1. Thomas Yoseloff, 1959.

Callahan, James M., *The Diplomatic History of the Southern Confederacy*. The Johns Hopkins Press, 1901.

Carrison, Daniel J., *The Navy from Wood to Steel, 1860-1890*. Franklin Watts, Inc., 1965.

Carse, Robert:
Blockade: The Civil War at Sea. Rinehart & Company, Inc., 1958.
Department of the South: Hilton Head Island in the Civil War. The State Printing Company, 1981.

Case, Lynn M., and Warren F. Spencer, *The United States and France: Civil War Diplomacy*. University of Pennsylvania Press, 1970.

Church, William Conant, *The Life of John Ericsson*. Charles Scribner's Sons, 1890.

Cochran, Hamilton, *Blockade Runners of the Confederacy*. The Bobbs-Merrill Company, Inc., 1958.

Coggins, Jack, *Arms and Equipment of the Civil War*. Doubleday & Company, Inc., 1962.

The Congressional Globe: The Debates and Proceedings of the Second Session of the Thirty-eighth Congress. Congressional Globe Office, 1865.

Conway's All the World's Fighting Ships, 1860-1905. Conway Maritime Press Ltd., 1979.

Copp, Elbridge J., *Reminiscences of the War of the Rebellion*. Telegraph Publishing Company, 1911.

Crook, D. P., *The North, the South and the Powers, 1861-1865*. John Wiley & Sons, 1974.

Daly, Robert W., ed:
Aboard the U.S.S. Monitor: 1862. United States Naval Institute, 1964.
How the Merrimac Won: The Strategic Story of the C.S.S. Virginia. Thomas Y. Crowell Company, 1957.

Dalzell, George W., *The Flight from the Flag*. The University of North Carolina Press, 1940.

Davis, William C., *Duel between the First Ironclads*. Louisiana State University Press, 1975.

Davis, William C., ed., *The Image of War, 1861-1865*:
Vol. 1, *Shadows of the Storm*. Doubleday & Co., Inc., 1981.
Vol. 2, *The Guns of '62*. Doubleday & Co., Inc., 1982.
Vol. 3, *The Embattled Confederacy*. Doubleday & Co., Inc., 1982.

Delaney, Norman C., *John McIntosh Kell of the Raider Alabama*. The University of Alabama Press, 1973.

Donovan, Frank R., *Ironclads of the Civil War*. American Heritage Publishing Co., Inc., 1964.

Duberman, Martin, *Charles Francis Adams, 1807-1886*. Stanford University Press, 1968.

Du Pont, H. A., *Rear-Admiral Samuel Francis Du Pont, United States Navy: A Biography*. National Americana Society, 1926.

Durkin, Joseph T., *Stephen R. Mallory: Confederate Navy Chief*. The University of North Carolina Press, 1954.

Eaton, Clement, *A History of the Southern Confederacy*. The Macmillan Company, 1954.

Ellicott, John M., *The Life of John Ancrum Winslow*. G. P. Putnam's Sons, 1902.

Ferris, Norman B., *The Trent Affair: A Diplomatic Crisis*. The University of Tennessee Press, 1977.

Foote, Shelby, *The Civil War, A Narrative: Red River to Appomattox*. Random House, 1974.

Gosnell, Harpur Allen, ed., *Rebel Raider: Being an Account of Raphael Semmes's Cruise in the C.S.S. Sumter*. The University of North Carolina Press, 1948.

Hill, Jim Dan:
The Civil War Sketchbook of Charles Ellery Stedman. Presidio Press, 1976.
Sea Dogs of the Sixties: Farragut and Seven Contemporaries. The University of Minnesota Press, 1935.

Hobart-Hampden, C. Augustus, *Never Caught: Personal Adventures Connected with Twelve Successful Trips in Blockade-Running During the American Civil War, 1863-1864*. The Blockade Runner Museum, 1967.

Horan, James D., ed., *C.S.S. Shenandoah: The Memoirs of Lieutenant Commanding James I. Waddell*. Crown Publishers, Inc., 1960.

Horn, Stanley F., *Gallant Rebel: The Fabulous Cruise of the C.S.S. Shenandoah*. Rutgers University Press, 1947.

Horner, Dave, *The Blockade-Runners: True Tales of Running the Yankee Blockade of the Confederate Coast*. Dodd, Mead & Company, 1968.

Hunt, C. E., *The Shenandoah, or the Last Confederate Cruiser*. G. W. Carleton & Co., 1867.

Hyman, Harold, ed., *Heard Round the World: The Impact Abroad of the Civil War*. Alfred A. Knopf, 1969.

Johnson, Robert Underwood, and Clarence Clough Buel, eds., *Battles and Leaders of the Civil War*, Vols. 1 and 4. Thomas Yoseloff, Inc., 1956.

Jones, Virgil Carrington, *The Civil War at Sea*, Vols. 1-3. Holt, Rinehart & Winston, 1960.

Jordan, Robert Paul, *The Civil War*. The National Geographic Society, 1969.

Kell, John McIntosh, *Recollections of a Naval Life*. The Neale Company, Publishers, 1900.

Kunhardt, Dorothy Meserve, and Philip B. Kunhardt Jr., *Mathew Brady and His World*. Time-Life Books, 1977.

Lester, Richard I., *Confederate Finance and Purchasing in Great Britain*. University Press of Virginia, 1975.

Long, E. B., with Barbara Long, *The Civil War Day by Day: An Almanac, 1861-1865*. Doubleday & Company, 1971.

Macartney, Clarence Edward, *Mr. Lincoln's Admirals*. Funk & Wagnalls Company, 1956.

MacBride, Robert, *Civil War Ironclads: The Dawn of Naval Armor*. Chilton Books, 1962.

McCordock, Robert Stanley, *The Yankee Cheese Box*. Dorrance and Company Publishers, 1938.

Macintyre, Donald, and Basil W. Bathe, *Man-of-War: A History of the Combat Vessel*. Gothenburg, Sweden: Tre Tryckare, Cagner & Co., 1969.

Maclay, Edgar Stanton, *A History of the United States Navy from 1775-1894*. D. Appleton and Company, 1897.

McPherson, James M., *Ordeal by Fire: The Civil War and Reconstruction*. Alfred A. Knopf, 1982.

Merli, Frank J., *Great Britain and the Confederate Navy, 1861-1865*. Indiana University Press, 1970.

Miller, Edward M., *U.S.S. Monitor: The Ship That Launched a Modern Navy*. Leeward Publications, Inc., 1978.

Miller, Nathan, *The U.S. Navy: An Illustrated History*. American Heritage Publishing Co., Inc., 1977.

Morgan, James Morris, *Recollections of a Rebel Reefer*. Houghton Mifflin Company, 1917.

Nash, Howard P., Jr., *A Naval History of the Civil War*. A. S. Barnes and Company, 1972.

Nevins, Allan, *The Improvised War, 1861-1862 (The War for the Union*, Vol. 1). Charles Scribner's Sons, 1959.

Niven, John, *Gideon Welles: Lincoln's Secretary of the Navy*. Oxford University Press, 1973.

Official Records of the Union and Confederate Navies in the War of the Rebellion. Government Printing Office, 1896.

Owsley, Frank Lawrence, Jr.:
The C.S.S. Florida: Her Building and Operations. University of Pennsylvania Press, 1965.
King Cotton Diplomacy: Foreign Relations of the Confederate States of America. The University of Chicago Press, 1959.

Patrick, Rembert W., *Jefferson Davis and His Cabinet*. Louisiana State University Press, 1944.

Potter, E. B., *United States Navy*. Galahad Books, 1971.

Randall, J. G., and David Donald, *The Divided Union*. Little, Brown and Company, 1961.

Reynolds, Clark G., *Command of the Sea: The History and Strategy of Maritime Empires*. William Morrow & Company, Inc., 1974.

Rimsky-Korsakoff, Nikolay Andreyevich, *My Musical Life*. Tudor Publishing Co., 1935.

Roberts, W. Adolphe, *Semmes of the Alabama*. The Bobbs-Merrill Company, 1938.

Robinson, William Morrison, Jr., *The Confederate Privateers*. Yale University Press, 1928.

Roland, Charles P., *The Confederacy*. The University of Chicago Press, 1960.

Roske, Ralph J., and Charles Van Doren, *Lincoln's Commando: The Biography of Commander W. B. Cushing, U.S.N.* Greenwood Press, Publishers, 1927.

Sandburg, Carl, *Abraham Lincoln: The War Years*, Vols. 1 and 3. Harcourt, Brace & Company, 1939.

Semmes, Raphael:
Service Afloat and Ashore during the Mexican War. Wm. H. Moore & Co., Publishers, 1851.

Service Afloat; or, The Remarkable Career of the Confederate Cruisers Sumter and Alabama during the War between the States. P. J. Kenedy and Sons.

Sideman, Belle Becker, and Lillian Friedman, eds., *Europe Looks at the Civil War.* The Orion Press, 1960.

Smith, Page, *Trial by Fire,* Vol. 5. McGraw-Hill Book Company, 1982.

Soley, James Russell, *The Blockade and the Cruisers.* Charles Scribner's Sons, 1883.

Sprout, Harold and Margaret, *The Rise of American Naval Power, 1776-1918.* Princeton University Press, 1939.

Sprunt, James, *Tales of the Cape Fear Blockade.* Clarendon Imprint, 1960.

Stern, Philip Van Doren, *The Confederate Navy: A Pictorial History.* Bonanza Books, 1962.

Still, William N., Jr., *Iron Afloat: The Story of the Confederate Armorclads.* Vanderbilt University Press, 1971.

Symonds, Craig L., ed., *Charleston Blockade: The Journals of John B. Marchand, U.S. Navy, 1861-1862.* Naval War College Press, 1976.

Taylor, Thomas E., *Running the Blockade: A Personal Narrative of Adventures, Risks, and Escapes during the American Civil War.* Books for Libraries Press, 1971.

Trexler, Harrison A., *The Confederate Ironclad "Virginia" ("Merrimac").* The University of Chicago Press, 1938.

United States Navy Department, Naval History Division: *Civil War Naval Chronology, 1861-1865.* U.S. Government Printing Office, 1971.

Dictionary of American Naval Fighting Ships, Vols. 1-8. U.S. Government Printing Office, 1959-1981.

United States Navy Department, Office of Naval War Records, *Officers in the Confederate States Navy, 1861-1865.* U.S. Government Printing Office, 1898.

Vandiver, Frank E., *Confederate Blockade Running through Bermuda, 1861-1865.* The University of Texas Press, 1947.

Vandiver, Frank E., ed., *Rebel Brass: The Confederate Command System.* Greenwood Press, Publishers, 1956.

Wallace, Sarah Agnes, and Frances Elma Gillespie, eds., *The Journal of Benjamin Moran: 1857-1865.* The University of Chicago Press, 1948.

Warren, Gordon H., *Fountain of Discontent: The Trent Affair and Freedom of the Seas.* Northeastern University Press, 1981.

Watts, Anthony J., *Pictorial History of the Royal Navy,* Vol. 1. London: Ian Allan, 1970.

Welles, Gideon, *Diary of Gideon Welles, Secretary of the Navy under Lincoln and Johnson.* Houghton Mifflin Company, 1911.

Wells, Tom Henderson, *The Confederate Navy: A Study in Organization.* The University of Alabama Press, 1971.

White, William Chapman and Ruth, *Tin Can on a Shingle.* E. P. Dutton & Company, Inc., 1957.

Wilkinson, John, *The Narrative of a Blockade-Runner.* Sheldon & Company, 1877.

Woldman, Albert A., *Lincoln and the Russians.* The World Publishing Company, 1952.

Other Sources

Delaney, Norman C., "The End of the *Alabama.*" *American Heritage,* April 1972.

"The Great Russian Ball." *Harper's Weekly,* November 21, 1863.

Hayes, John D., "Sea Power in the Civil War." *United States Naval Institute Proceedings,* November 1961.

Heffernan, John B., "The Blockade of the Southern Confederacy: 1861-1865." *The Smithsonian Journal of History,* Winter 1967-1968.

"Honors to the Russian Naval Officers." *The New York Times,* October 2, 1863.

Johnson, Ludwell H., "Commerce between Northeastern Ports and the Confederacy, 1861-1865." *The Journal of American History,* June 1967.

Long, James C., "The Poorest Ironclad in the Confederacy: An Officer's Opinion of the *Albemarle.*" *Civil War Times Illustrated,* January 1975.

O'Flaherty, Daniel, "The Blockade That Failed." *American Heritage,* August 1955.

"Our Russian Visitors." *Harper's Weekly,* October 17, 1863.

"Rear-Admiral Lisovski, of the Russian Navy." *Frank Leslie's Illustrated Newspaper,* November 7, 1863.

"The Russian Ball." *Harper's Weekly,* November 21, 1863.

"The Russian Banquet." *The New York Times,* October 20, 1863.

"The Russian Fleet in New York Harbor." *Frank Leslie's Illustrated Newspaper,* October 24, 1863.

PICTURE CREDITS

The sources for the illustrations that appear in this book are listed below. Credits for the illustrations from left to right are separated by semicolons; from top to bottom they are separated by dashes.

Cover: Peabody Museum of Salem, photographed by Mark Sexton. 2, 3: Map by Peter McGinn. 8, 9: War Memorial of Virginia. 11: The New Jersey Historical Society, photographed by Henry Groskinsky. 12: Library of Congress. 13: United States Naval Academy/Beverley R. Robinson Collection. 15: Courtesy Philip Kunhardt. 18, 19: John Batchelor. 20: National Portrait Gallery, Smithsonian Institution, Washington, D.C. — Library of Congress. 22, 23: Photograph from the Samuel H. Lockett Papers in the Southern Historical Collection, the University of North Carolina. 25: Library of Congress. 26, 27: Courtesy Mystic Seaport Museum — courtesy Frank Wood. 29: National Archives. 30: From *The Navies* (*The Photographic History of the Civil War,* Vol. 6) by James Barnes, The Review of Reviews Co., 1912. 32, 33: United States Naval Academy/Beverley R. Robinson Collection. 34, 35: Library of Congress. 36-39: The Western Reserve Historical Society. 40, 41: Military History Institute, Carlisle Barracks, Pa., copied by Robert Walch, insets: Library of Congress; The Western Reserve Historical Society. 42, 43: New Hampshire Historical Society; Military History Institute, Carlisle Barracks, Pa., copied by Robert Walch — The New Jersey Historical Society, copied by Henry Groskinsky. 44, 45: New Hampshire Historical Society, inset, Library of Congress. 47: U.S. Navy Photo, courtesy The Mariners' Museum, Newport News, Va. 50: The Chrysler Museum. 52, 53: From *Battles and Leaders of the Civil War,* The Century Co., New York. 54: Courtesy of The New-York Historical Society, New York. 56, 57: U.S. Navy Photo; Library of Congress; courtesy The Mariners' Museum, Newport News, Va.; U.S.

Naval Academy Museum. 58, 59: Courtesy Jay P. Altmayer, photographed by Larry Cantrell. 60: Library of Congress. 61: Courtesy The Mariners' Museum, Newport News, Va. 63: U.S. Naval Academy/Beverley R. Robinson Collection. 64: Courtesy Frank Wood. 66, 67: Courtesy The Mariners' Museum, Newport News, Va. 68, 69: Courtesy The Mariners' Museum, Newport News, Va.; U.S. Navy Photo. 70, 71: Military History Institute, Carlisle Barracks, Pa., copied by Robert Walch. 72, 73: Courtesy Charles S. Schwartz; U.S. Navy Photo. 74, 75: Library of Congress; National Archives Neg. No. 111-B-611. 76, 77: Library of Congress. 78, 79: Courtesy Frank Wood, insets: from *History of the Confederate States Navy* by J. Thomas Scharf, published by The Fairfax Press; Military History Institute, Carlisle Barracks, Pa., copied by Robert Walch. 80, 81: Culver Pictures, Inc. 82, 83: Culver Pictures, Inc. (2); courtesy Paul De Haan. 84, 85: Courtesy of The New-York Historical Society, New York. 87: Museum of the Confederacy, photographed by Larry Sherer. 89: West Point Museum Collection, United States Military Academy. 90, 91: U.S. Navy Photo, courtesy The Mariners' Museum, Newport News, Va. — courtesy Frank Wood. 92, 93: Private collection. 95: North Carolina State Archives. 97: Library of Congress. 99: Nassau Public Library, Bahamas. 100: Library of Congress. 102, 103: Military History Institute, Carlisle Barracks, Pa., copied by Robert Walch (2) — Military History Institute, Carlisle Barracks, Pa. (2). 104, 105: Military History Institute, Carlisle Barracks, Pa., except top right. 106, 107: Military History Institute, Carlisle Barracks, Pa., copied by Robert Walch; Military History Institute, Carlisle Barracks, Pa. 108, 109: Military History Institute, Carlisle Barracks, Pa., copied by Robert Walch; Military History Institute, Carlisle Barracks, Pa. (2). 110-113: Military History Institute, Carlisle Barracks, Pa. 115: From *History of the Confederate States Navy* by J. Thomas Scharf, published by The Fair-

fax Press. 117: Courtesy The Mariners' Museum, Newport News, Va. 119: Courtesy William Gladstone. 121: Library of Congress. 123: Courtesy Williamson Art Gallery and Museum, Birkenhead, England, photographed by Hal Mullin. 124, 125: Chicago Historical Society. 126: Courtesy Philip Kunhardt. 127: U.S. Department of the Interior, National Park Service, Adams National Historical Site, Quincy, Mass. 129: Imperial War Museum, London — The National Maritime Museum, London. 130: Library of Congress. 132, 133: The Naval Museum, Leningrad; except portrait, National Portrait Gallery, Smithsonian Institution, Washington, D.C. 134, 135: Courtesy Frank Wood. 136, 137: The Naval Museum, Leningrad. 138, 139: Courtesy Frank Wood. 140, 141: The Naval Museum, Leningrad (2); Library of Congress. 143: Military History Institute, Carlisle Barracks, Pa., copied by Robert Walch. 144, 145: The Peabody Museum of Salem, photographed by Mark Sexton. 147: The Huntington Library, San Marino, Calif. 148: The Metropolitan Museum of Art, The Harris Brisbane Dick Fund, 1929. 150: Museum of the Confederacy — courtesy Frank Wood. 151: National Archives, Record Group No. 45 — American Heritage Publishing Company. 153: U.S. Navy Photo, Neg. No. NH57256. 154: Map by William L. Hezlep. 156: U.S. Naval Academy Museum, Annapolis, Md. 158: U.S. Navy Photo, courtesy The Mariners' Museum, Newport News, Va. 159: Museum of the Confederacy — The Washington Light Infantry of Charleston, S.C., photographed by Harold H. Norvell. 162, 163: National Archives, Neg. No. 111-B-448; U.S. Navy. 164, 165: The Union League Club of New York, photographed by Paulus Leeser. 166, 167: Philadelphia Museum of Art/The John G. Johnson Collection; American Heritage Publishing Company. 168, 169: U.S. Naval Academy/ Beverley R. Robinson Collection. 170, 171: Chicago Historical Society, Neg. No. 1947.5.

ACKNOWLEDGMENTS

The editors thank the following individuals and institutions for their help in the preparation of this volume:

Florida: Pensacola—Norman Simons, Pensacola Historical Society Museum.

Maryland: Annapolis—James Cheevers, U.S. Naval Academy Museum; Sigrid Trumpy, the Beverley R. Robinson Collection, U.S. Naval Academy Museum. Camp Springs—Captain Ernest W. Peterkin, U.S.N. (Ret.).

Pennsylvania: Carlisle Barracks—Michael Winey, U.S. Army Military History Institute. Philadelphia—Peter Sutton, Philadelphia Museum of Art.

Virginia: Newport News—Lois Oglesby, Charlotte Valentine, Mariners' Museum. Richmond—Cathy Carlson, Museum of the Confederacy.

Washington, D.C.: Robert A. Carlisle, Still Photo Branch, Navy Office of Information; Howard Hoffman, Division of Naval History, National Museum of American History; John Reilly, Naval Historical Center, Washington Navy Yard; William Stapp, National Portrait Gallery.

The index for this book was prepared by Nicholas J. Anthony.

INDEX